THE MAN WHO WAS
PRESIDENT
FOR A DAY

AND OTHER INSPIRING STORIES
ABOUT THE PRESIDENTS

Andrew McCrea

BLAKE
& KING

Maysville, Missouri

Published by Blake and King
5650 Berlin Road
Maysville, MO 64469

Publisher's Cataloguing-in-Publication Data
McCrea, Andrew.

   The Man Who Was President for a Day : and other inspiring stories about the presidents / Andrew McCrea. — Maysville, MO : Blake and King, 2004.

p. ; cm.
An intriguing look at life and leadership through unique stories about the American presidents.
ISBN: 0-9725331-1-7

1. Presidents—United States—Anecdotes. I. Title.

E176.1 .M33 2004   2004104382
973/.09/9—dc22   0406

Book production and coordination by Jenkins Group, Inc. • www.bookpublishing.com

Interior design by Paw Print Media/Debbie Sidman
Cover design by Kelli Leader

Printed in the United States of America

08 07 06 05 04 • 5 4 3 2 1

Dedication

To my mother, who challenged me to learn the names of the presidents, and to my father, who drove the family car to so many of their homes.

Acknowledgments

Many people have played an important role in making the chapters of this book a reality. The staff of each presidential site were knowledgeable, friendly, and took the extra time to conduct interviews and provide valuable insights into the lives of those profiled.

Portions of these chapters were first heard as features on my daily radio program, *American Countryside*. Tom Brand, editor of the program, has played a vital role in compiling the original interviews into the features our listeners hear.

The Brownfield Network and Learfield Communications based in Jefferson City, Missouri, as well as the staff of KFEQ radio in St. Joseph, Missouri, have also provided the assistance needed to gather and share the stories in this book and have broadcast *American Countryside* from its inception. Without their support, this book and our daily broadcasts would not be possible. I also wish to thank the many radio stations who air our program and the listeners who make it possible.

To the dedicated teachers of King City High School who provided me with a wonderful place to grow and learn, I thank you.

My parents and family have provided love, support, and strength. I thank God for all of these people in my life and the opportunity to share a few of these stories with others.

And . . . to the people I've met as I "travel the countryside" who inspire the stories and teach life's lessons along the way, I thank you.

Contents

The Journey Begins
KING CITY, MISSOURI

"When you get to be president, there are all those things, the honors, the twenty-one gun salutes, all those things. You have to remember it isn't for you. It's for the presidency."

—HARRY TRUMAN

I t all began with some Wonder Bread wrappers, a twelve-inch ruler, and a challenge from my mother. As I look back, it's hard to imagine such a strange combination could ever produce a book, much less anything else of note.

I don't know why I was interested in the presidents of the United States when I was in second grade. I can't remember us taking much time to study the topic in class, although I do remember an article in our *Weekly Reader* about the 1980 presidential election. That particular race was not the type of close contest that would inspire a young man to dig into the subject, as Ronald Reagan easily defeated incumbent Jimmy Carter 489 to 49 in the electoral vote. I remember our class held a mock vote prior to the election and that Reagan won that contest, too. I also recall voting for Carter, which didn't make me popular with my classmates, but I knew it was what both of my deeply Democratic grandfathers would have wanted me to do.

Somewhere in the midst of that lopsided presidential election, I was inspired to learn more about these men we were voting on at school. When my mom found out what was going on, she told me how she'd had to memorize the names of all the presidents, in order, for a class she'd taken back in high school. Leave it to me; I was just the kind of kid who would want to do something like that while I was in the second grade.

That's where a twelve-inch ruler came oddly into the picture. At the time, a local company gave all second graders a wooden ruler as part of our school supplies. On the back of each ruler was a list of the presidents. That was all the fuel I needed. Armed with the challenge from my mother and a ruler that listed all their names, I began slowly committing those names to memory every few minutes I had to spare in class.

My teacher, Mrs. Herbster, probably through an off-hand comment made by my mother in a parent-teacher conference, heard about my efforts. One day she asked me how I was coming along memorizing the names of the presidents, undoubtedly figuring I'd make a good stab at it and would get six or seven names into the list. I remember standing there beside her desk and rattling off the entire list in perfect order, concluding with Ronald Reagan, the man I had spurned in our classroom vote. I think she was shocked that an eight-year-old stood before her and accomplished the task. In any event, I eventually got to the point where I could speedily recite the list in a mere ten seconds.

Mrs. Herbster was a great teacher. She taught me in both first and second grades and she decided that my efforts should be rewarded. At the time, the Wonder Bread Company was packing baseball card-sized cutouts of the presidents in their loaves of bread. She had been saving those trading cards at her home, but when she found out I had memorized the names of all the presidents, she gave me her collection. That was quite a gift! Not one other kid in my class would have cared about those cards, but they were like gold to me. I put them in my desk but peeked at one or two of them whenever no one was watching.

I trace everything in this book back to that experience in second grade, though other events through the years continued to shape my interest in the topic. There was the occasional summer vacation (always fewer than five days in length so Dad would not miss too many farm chores!) that allowed for a stop at a presidential site. The first stop was at the Truman Library in Independence, Missouri, the closest site to our home.

By the time I was in college, I was able to experience politics "for real" when I served as a legislative intern for Representative Phil Tate in the Missouri General Assembly. He took the time to thoroughly explain the political process to me, often taking a break to sit with me along the side gallery on the assembly floor to discuss why and how the system did and didn't work.

In the summer of 1994, I finally got to visit the place where most of our former presidents had lived. As national secretary for the National FFA Organization (once known by its full name, Future Farmers of America), our six-member national officer team traveled to the White House to listen to President Bill Clinton record one of his Saturday morning radio addresses. We then got to go through a receiving line and visit with the president himself in the Oval Office. I was twenty-one years old, and I remember telling myself, "Take a real good look at everything in here because this is probably the only time you're ever gonna see it in person."

The president treated the six of us national officers very cordially. Oddly enough, besides his friendly conversation, the thing I remember most about the event was his watch. He stood before us wearing a finely tailored dark suit, the kind of suit with threads that gleamed bright, even in the dimmest light. But as he reached out to shake our hands, I noticed he was wearing a digital watch with a black plastic wristband. It looked like the type of watch you could pick up for a couple of dollars on a discount rack and seemed out of place in comparison with that suit.

When our turn in the receiving line was over, the president turned to those waiting and said, "If more young people were a part of that group, we wouldn't have nearly the problems we have today." Clinton had attended the state FFA convention in his home state of Arkansas several times when he was governor, and I appreciated what he had to say.

Although by 2001 I had been visiting presidential sites for several years, I began to make an effort to capture radio interviews at every presidential site possible for a series of programs that appeared on the *American Countryside* radio broadcasts. Those features later became the basis for this book.

As I've written these chapters, I've kept in mind the fact that many people think they don't like history, let alone reading about presidents. Thus, this book is not a boring encyclopedic version of each president's term in office. The goal of the presidential radio series and of this book is to make presidential history fun and informative.

I personally traveled to all the sites mentioned. Although I interviewed a great variety of presidential experts and pored over many books and writings, you will usually find only one person quoted in each chapter. This is not because anyone did a poor job relaying their part of history but because to list more would make these chapters read like book reports. On the contrary, these stories are intended to be conversational and to focus on the positive. Better yet, I hope they reveal insights you can carry into the present to make the most of the future.

Winston Churchill once said, "The farther back you can look, the farther forward you can see." It is important to examine history so we can both avoid the mistakes of the past and apply positive lessons that will affect the future. This book intentionally brings out the positive points of our presidents. While each president can be held accountable for errors in judgment, our twenty-first century perspective also gives us 20/20 vision when it comes to evaluating other aspects of their lives and their presidencies.

As you read these stories, you may find they hold different leadership lessons for you than they did for me. Great! I hope you enjoy the features, but I also hope that, like me, you take home a lesson you might use in life.

You will find that the point, or moral, of each story is included in a shaded box with a compass symbol. The first compasses were used by the Chinese almost two thousand years ago. They used lodestones, a mineral composed of iron oxide, that aligns itself in a north-south direction. These natural magnets were eventually placed on squares with directional markings. Once navigators found north, they immediately knew how to find east, south, and west.

The shaded boxes in this book work much the same as a compass. These simple points are designed to give our lives direction. As we begin to apply these lessons to our lives, we will be better able to navigate the challenges we encounter every day. These boxes are part of the original story, yet they are highlighted to emphasize the "direction" they can provide us.

What Happened to Eisenhower?

You will notice that the last president featured in this book is Harry Truman. You may say, "What about Eisenhower, Kennedy, Johnson, and so forth? Why aren't the most recent presidents included?" There is a very simple reason for this: you already know too much! Imagine that I were to write a chapter about Jimmy Carter (yes, my choice back in second grade) and you are a die-hard Republican who hates every policy Carter ever stood for. No matter what nice things I write about President Carter, you will say I don't have any idea what I'm talking about.

Now imagine that I've written a fun and informative chapter about President Chester Arthur. Unless you are a history professor, you just might say, "A guy named Chester Arthur was really president?" Harry Truman died the same year I was born. In a way, this book is a look back at the presidents I didn't know first-hand.

How were these stories collected?

If you've never heard the *American Countryside* radio broadcasts, they are a daily three-minute feature that highlights fascinating people and places and tells their interesting stories. We bill these broadcasts as a "slice of Americana," similar to what journalist Charles Kuralt used to produce for television.

Almost every interview is a result of me being in an area to speak or to present a workshop. I use the phrase "in an area" very loosely. For instance, in gathering the stories for this book, I was once in Washington, D.C., for a leadership conference and figured that Buffalo, New York, could be considered "in the area." Certainly Buffalo is much closer to D.C. than it is to my home and farm north of Kansas City, Missouri.

Although I do spend some time on the road speaking to groups and traveling to gather radio features, I still live on the farm in northwest Missouri where I grew up. In fact, I spend the majority of my time farming with my father (although he seems to think I have an uncanny knack for leaving on a trip just as the weather clears enough for us to go bale hay). I also continue to present programs to youth and adults from a variety of organizations. This book has proven to be a presidential journey that has taught me a lot about life, thanks to the lessons shared by the people and places I've met while traveling the countryside.

A Fourth of July to Forget

FARMINGTON, PENNSYLVANIA

*"We ought not to look back unless it is to derive useful
lessons from past errors, and for the purpose of profiting
by dear-bought experience."*

—GEORGE WASHINGTON

Did you know George Washington . . .

...PROBABLY DIDN'T LIKE THE EVENTS OF THE FOURTH OF JULY?

...ESCAPED DEATH BY SURRENDERING HIS ARMY WHEN HE WAS ONLY
TWENTY-TWO YEARS OLD?

...LEARNED IMPORTANT LESSONS AT A WILDERNESS FORT THAT LATER
HELPED HIM WIN THE WAR FOR INDEPENDENCE?

Before our nation's war for independence, a different war opened the door to the west for a country yet to be born. This is a conflict many have forgotten, yet this series of battles provided the experience a young man needed to someday lead a new nation to victory.

Americans sometimes forget that many historically significant events occurred well before the thirteen colonies decided to declare their independence. For some of us, our history clock begins on

July 4, 1776, and any event before this date is automatically insignificant. We perhaps don't intend to take this view, but we often unconsciously forget about the events that helped the new country shake European rule.

The year was 1753, and young George Washington, seeking to gain experience and recognition in the Virginia militia, requested that the state governor send him on an expedition deep into the frontier to deliver a summons to the French occupying lands east of the Appalachian Mountains. That letter asserted British rights to the territory and declared that all others should leave the area. Governor Dinwiddie of Virginia had learned that the French had built forts on frontier lands claimed by the colony of Virginia, and Washington's eight-member party ordered the withdrawal of those French forces.

One letter from an unknown twenty-year-old Virginian named George Washington wasn't going to convince anyone to leave land they believed was rightfully theirs, and the refusal of the French to depart set the stage for a conflict between the world's superpowers, the British and the French. In 1754, even before Governor Dinwiddie had learned of France's refusal to leave, he sent a detachment of men to erect a fort near present-day Pittsburgh. The small fort was barely finished when the French drove out the Virginians, claimed the structure for themselves, expanded the walls, and called it Fort Duquesne.

In April of that same year, Washington was again sent back toward present-day western Maryland and southwestern Pennsylvania, this time to carve out a road that would bring troops to roust out the French. By May 24, 1754, Washington had reached a large, open swampy area called the Great Meadows near present-day Farmington, Pennsylvania, a place he deemed "a charming field for an encounter."

Just three days later, Washington learned that a group of French were about seven miles away and he quickly gathered forty men to go with him to track them down. Using the element of surprise,

Washington quickly defeated the enemy, but one of the French escaped to tell his larger force that the British colonials were in the area and on the offensive. Realizing that he had in effect awakened what could be a sleeping giant of an army that could easily swarm his small force, Washington headed back to the Great Meadows to build a fort. To use the term "fort" is generous; it was actually just a small, circular stockade only fifty-three feet in diameter. He called it his "fort of necessity." It was where Washington would get his first true taste of leading an army under siege.

Within just a few days, six hundred French marines and militia along with one hundred Indian allies had surrounded Washington's 290 Virginians plus one hundred British soldiers from South Carolina. Not only was he outnumbered, Colonel Washington wrote that his troops were "Loose idle men destitute of house and home." Most were on the road-building assignment to earn the free land that was promised in payment. The battle that ensued on July 3, 1754, lasted about eight hours with most of the gunfire taking place in a pouring rain.

Brian Reedy, a ranger at Fort Necessity National Battlefield, the site where that skirmish took place, says that Washington's fort was "just upright stakes or poles of white oak that were split in half with small dividers between the larger posts for muskets to fit through." Washington built earthworks around the fort to help defend it as well, but after eight hours, the tide was turning against him. About thirty of his men had been killed with another seventy wounded. The trenches that had been built around the fort as a place from which to fire at the enemy were now filled with water. Of those still able to fight, several had broken into the rum supply and were now drunk. When the French offered Washington the chance to surrender, he took them up on the offer. That surrender took place on July 4 and marked the only time he would ever surrender an army.

The event made an impact on Washington, one he reflected upon after the colonies declared their independence twenty-two years later on July 4. On July 20, 1776, Washington wrote to Adam Stephen, fellow officer in the American army and one of several Virginians to be with him at Fort Necessity, "I did not let the anniversary...pass without a grateful remembrance of the escape we had at the Meadows [Ft. Necessity 1754]..." Reedy explains that Washington was in effect saying, "Here we are becoming a country on July 4th and yet I was lucky to escape with my life on July 4th back in 1754."

Washington saw value in looking back at the events in one's life, yet he said, "We ought not to look back unless it is to derive useful lessons from past errors, and for the purpose of profiting by dear-bought experience." Fort Necessity provided just that. Reedy explains, "He would go on to lose many more battles, but he always found himself on the winning side. The thing he learned from Fort Necessity was to never have himself totally surrounded, to find some way to escape."

That strategy became important during the Revolutionary War, especially during the New York City campaign, when Washington was defeated in battle after battle but somehow found a way to keep his army together and take on the British army. "His real skill was not fighting; his real skill was keeping an army intact and he did that quite well. He didn't win many battles, but he won the war," says Reedy. Thanks in part to looking back, a fourth of July to forget provided the experience for a fourth of July to remember twenty-two years later.

Defending the Undefendable
BOSTON, MASSACHUSETTS

*"Facts are stubborn things; and whatever may be our wishes,
our inclinations, or the dictates of our passions, they cannot alter
the state of facts, and evidence."*

—JOHN ADAMS

Did you know John Adams . . .

...WAS PART OF A FAMOUS STORY THAT BEGAN WITH ONE SNOWBALL?

...CRITICIZED A MAN WHO IS CONSIDERED THE FIRST PATRIOT TO DIE
FOR INDEPENDENCE?

...HAD TO DEFEND ONE OF THE MOST UNPOPULAR GROUPS OF MEN IN
THE CITY OF BOSTON?

Samuel Gray, James Coldwell, Samuel Maverick, and Patrick Carr. Those names don't mean much to people today, and it is perhaps only the addition of the last name to the group of five, Crispus Attucks, that provides a clue to the men's identity. Nonetheless, these five men were at the center of a defining moment in the colonies' fight for independence and one future president's life.

"It was not a massacre at all . . . it was essentially a riot," says Rick Wiggin, executive director of the Bostonian Society, an organization whose offices have an aerial view of the site where those men became famous in 1770. Although today we know the event as the "Boston Massacre," the facts of that night may be far different than what many believe.

In the years before the colonies declared their independence, tensions ran high in the city of Boston. Citizens were weary of the taxes placed upon them by King George and they grew resentful of the British soldiers who had become an occupying force in their city. Those feelings exploded on the night of March 5, 1770. Ironically, it was a snowball that lit the fuse for an event still seen as a rallying point for the patriot cause.

The accounts of that night differ, but most agree it all began with a confrontation between a lone customs house sentry, Private Hugh White, and a boy named Edward Garrick. It wasn't unusual for British soldiers like White to hear taunts and jeers from Bostonians, but Garrick's heckling that night may even have been laced with a few snowballs lobbed at the guard. Eventually the soldier had heard enough and lashed out with the butt of his gun. The boy, now feeling he was in a fight bigger than himself, ran to gather his friends, who offered a larger barrage of words and snowballs.

With the fuse now lit, the scene grew ever closer to its explosion. Reinforcements were called to defend the customs house. Meanwhile, church bells rang, not to signal worship, but to call people into the streets. A mob formed in front of the customs house with many citizens tossing snowballs, often packed with stones in their interior, toward the troops.

Wiggin says at least some of the townspeople did fear the barrage of snow and ice might draw retaliation in the form of gunfire from the Brits led by Captain Thomas Preston. "Preston had just assured one citizen that they weren't going to fire because he was standing in front of his troops. He was saying, 'Look, if they're going to fire, they're going to hit me!'"

Soon Private Hugh Montgomery was knocked to the ground by a stone-laced snowball and, in the ensuing seconds, someone did fire. Wiggins explains, "In self-defense, the troops simply fired to protect themselves. It was over very quickly and not in any way a massacre. It was simply a riot." Nonetheless, five men died, and Sam Adams and other "radicals" in Boston seized the moment as a rallying point, declaring the troops had needlessly fired into the innocent assembly.

The next day, Captain Preston and eight other troops were accused of murder. The expectation was that they would all quickly be found guilty. Wiggin adds, "It occurred in a very radicalized town and so the sentiments of all the townspeople were in favor of the rioters, and the soldiers were immediately looked at as perpetrators."

Most people have seen the famous Paul Revere engraving of the event published in many history books. The depiction was itself a propaganda piece. It inaccurately shows the troops firing in unison at the command of Preston. The customs house in front of which the event occurred is even renamed "Butcher's Hall" in the picture.

To most Americans, that's where the story ends. We've heard of the Boston Massacre, but most of us don't know there is another chapter to the story, an epilogue in which a lawyer named John Adams stepped forward to defend the villainous soldiers. Adams was considered the foremost attorney at the time in Boston, and it was he, along with Josiah Quincy, who led the defense of those men.

Just imagine it: here you have a future president of the United States defending a group that Bostonians considered undefendable. "I think if John Adams' credentials as a 'radical' had not been well established, he would have been lynched," says Wiggin. However, Wiggin explains, "John Adams believed passionately in the integrity of the legal system and the importance of giving these soldiers a fair trial."

Today, history books regard Crispus Attucks, a black man, as an American hero, and some claim him as the first patriot to be killed in the Revolution, although it would be six more years before the colonies would formally declare their independence. John Adams, however, did not regard Attucks as a hero. Instead, in his defense of the British soldiers, he declared, "This was the behavior of Attucks, to whose mad behavior, in all probability, the dreadful carnage of that night, is chiefly to be ascribed."

In that December 1770 trial Adams further declared, "Facts are stubborn things; and whatever may be our wishes, our inclinations, or the dictates of our passion, they cannot alter the state of facts and evidence." It is hard to imagine a future president speaking out against Attucks, a man who today is considered a great patriot, yet Adams was a man of principle and he was not afraid to speak his mind, even when he knew it would make him unpopular.

Caroline Kineth, deputy superintendent at the Adam's National Historic Site, says of John Adams and his son John Quincy, "They were two men who believed greatly in their country and were willing to sacrifice themselves, their family, everything in order to serve the country, and they would not compromise one iota if they didn't feel it was the right thing to do. They weren't in it to serve themselves; they were in it to serve the country."

Character and conscience led John Adams to defend the "unde-fendable" in Boston, taking an unpopular stand in a difficult time. While Adams has sometimes been overlooked since his presidential term is sandwiched between heroes Washington and Jefferson, today he is rightfully receiving renewed attention because of those values for which he stood.

Cultivating Liberty
CHARLOTTESVILLE, VIRGINIA

*"The greatest service which can be rendered any country
is to add a useful plant to its culture."*

—THOMAS JEFFERSON

Did you know Thomas Jefferson . . .

...GREW OVER THREE HUNDRED VARIETIES OF VEGETABLES AT HIS
HOME DURING HIS LIFETIME?

...SMUGGLED RICE FROM EUROPE DESPITE THE PENALTY OF DEATH?

...WROTE OVER ONE THOUSAND PAGES ABOUT THE CROPS AND
GARDENS HE GREW?

There are many contributions Thomas Jefferson made to his country. For most Americans, it is the words he penned to open the Declaration of Independence that are his greatest legacy. Many people believe Jefferson also played a key role in writing the U.S. Constitution in 1787. However, he was not even close to where those delegates convened. Where was he? In Europe, smuggling rice under penalty of death!

Of course, that is a bit of an overstatement, but it is one of the things Jefferson accomplished while serving as the American minister to France. We know much of Jefferson's accomplishments as a founding father and third president of the nation. About a half million visitors tour his home of Monticello every year to learn more about his life. But when visitors arrive, they may just be struck by Jefferson's great love for farming and gardening.

Peter Hatch, director of gardens and grounds at Monticello, says, "Jefferson always aspired to a certain self-sufficiency in terms of agriculture. He was also a great experimenter. Jefferson said, 'The greatest service which can be rendered any country is to add a useful plant to its culture.'" It was this philosophy that influenced the way he ran his five-thousand-acre farm near Charlottesville, Virginia.

Today, land grant universities have a mission to perform agricultural research. They receive government funding to do studies that will aid farmers in growing better crops and livestock. In the late 1700s and early 1800s, Thomas Jefferson performed that task for the farmers of the young nation. While experimental studies such as those Jefferson conducted are very valuable in the knowledge they provide, they are rarely profitable. That may in part be why Jefferson's farm fell deeply into debt by the time of his death in 1826.

Hatch says, "Jefferson documented the planting of 330 varieties of vegetables and 170 varieties of fruit." Today, Hatch oversees the same land that Jefferson once cultivated. He has an incredible guide for the task, since Jefferson left behind two important diaries, one called the "Garden Book" and the other the "Farm Book. Together, they contain over one thousand pages of detailed accounts of what, where, and when crops were sown.

It was while Jefferson was serving as the American minister to France that he had time to explore the surrounding regions. Part of that journey took him over the Alps into northern Italy. There he found upland rice flourishing (upland rice is rice that does not require excessively wet ground or "swamps" in order to be grown). He thought this rice might grow well in the United States and wanted to ship some home.

Local officials forbid the unhusked rice to be taken from their region to prevent other countries from growing the crop and competing against them. The penalty for such smuggling was death. In a letter to Edward Rutledge, Jefferson wrote, "I determined to take enough [rice] to put you in seed: they informed me, however, its exportation in the husk was prohibited; so I could only bring off as much as my coat and pockets would hold." Hatch says of the seed, "Upland rice really never took on in this country, but it was sort of typical of Jefferson's experimental efforts to reform agriculture."

Thomas Jefferson was one of the founders of the county agricultural society. He introduced the rotation of crops and contour plowing to his farm, a practice soon adopted by other farmers. In 1794 Jefferson introduced a new invention, a moldboard for a plow. "People have traditionally thought of Jefferson as a great inventor, but in fact his only real invention was a moldboard, which won agricultural medals in Paris in the 1800s," says Hatch. This moldboard plow sliced through the ground more easily, allowing land to be more efficiently cultivated.

In his first inaugural address in 1801, Jefferson spoke of the bountiful land he dreamed the United States would become. He foresaw "a rising nation, spread over a wide and fruitful land, advancing rapidly to destinies beyond the reach of mortal eye." Jefferson commissioned the Lewis and Clark expedition in January of 1803, months before the U.S. acquired the Louisiana Purchase. But when the expedition departed St. Louis on May 14, 1804, the territory was a part of the nation, and the expedition set out to explore the territory and journey all the way to the Pacific Ocean. The adventure provided a wealth of new plant and animal species for Jefferson to examine, including Mandan corn and Arikara beans from the Native Americans, which he began to grow in his own Monticello gardens.

So much can be said about Jefferson and the impact he made in so many different areas of life. Hatch says, "He's not easily described and I think that's why he is such a great early American figure, because he can represent so much and it's so difficult to pin down his legacy; it's sort of endless in a lot of ways." Jefferson's devotion to agriculture proves just that. Few Americans know of the great contributions he made in the fields of botany, agronomy, and conservation, yet they represent major interests in his life.

Jefferson surrounded himself with a variety of interests and allowed his mind to explore. While in France, he wrote, "I am constantly roving about to see what I have never seen before and shall never see again." It was that spirit that led him to leave so many contributions in so many areas. Just as Jefferson planted new seeds to watch them sprout and grow, our thirst to explore and learn should flourish as well.

The Dynamic Duo
Montpelier Station, Virginia

"Conscience is the most sacred of all property."

—James Madison

Did you know James Madison . . .

...Is often referred to as the "Father of the Constitution"?
...Was married to one of the most famous of First Ladies?
...Was the shortest president at 5' 4"?

"In one sense he was an unlikely member of that group of founding fathers. He was a short man, he was not a military hero, he was somewhat shy; we might call him a 'bookworm,'" says Randy Huwa, past communications director at Montpelier, home of fourth president James Madison. He noted that Madison was only 5' 4" and his voice was less than commanding, yet when people heard his ideas, they realized he was a man who was well read and someone whose ideas often served to bring sides together.

James Madison grew up in central Virginia on his family's farm. He studied at what is today Princeton University and then returned home to study law. He had little taste for the topic, but when religious persecution of Baptists and other denominations occurred in nearby Culpepper County, he found passion in defending the religious freedoms of these Virginians. In 1780 at the age of twenty-nine, he became the youngest member of the Continental Congress.

By 1786, the young nation was in turmoil. The lack of a strong national government under the Articles of Confederation led to a call for changes in the document or a completely new constitution. In May of 1787, the Constitutional Convention convened with George Washington as its chair. It was Madison who was behind the "Virginia Plan," which created two legislative chambers, the lower of which was based on the population of the states, with the other chamber filled with two senators from each state. Madison emerged as the leader of the proceedings.

"What he brought to the Constitutional Convention in 1787 was an enormous amount of knowledge about what had happened and what had been tried in earlier forms of government. He really was a walking encyclopedia," says Huwa. He had consumed all the knowledge he could about other nations and their forms of government. "He certainly was the guiding light of that Constitutional Convention, and it's for that reason that his contemporaries called him the 'Father of the Constitution.'"

In 1794, at the age of forty-three, he married twenty-six-year-old Dolly Payne Todd, a widow with an infant son. Huwa says of the couple, "Opposites attract, and in many ways they were very different, but they were a great partnership." She did seem to be the opposite of her husband. She was a vivacious lady described by author Washington Irving as "a fine, portly buxom dame." She was an excellent hostess and when she served pastry shells filled with ice cream, they became known as Dolly Madison cakes. Her name is still the brand name for pastry treats today.

Later, as first lady, her social skills became even more valuable. Huwa says, "Dolly would often put political opponents at the same table at one of her dinner parties because she recognized that if people found something to agree on and grew familiar with one another and learned a little bit more about each other, compromise was easier to come by."

When Thomas Jefferson was elected president in 1800, Madison became his secretary of state. Eight years later, after Jefferson's two terms as president, James Madison was elected as the fourth president of the United States. During his first four years in office, several factors led to strained relations with Britain and eventually to war. For one thing, Britain interfered with American shipping interests, while American settlers in the northwest territories (in the area of Ohio and Indiana today) were under attack from a league of Indians led by Tecumseh, who was aided by the British.

By 1812, a group of pro-war congressmen known as the War Hawks were leading the effort to declare war on Britain. They wanted to expand the country's borders north into Canada, south in Florida, and gain solid control of the west. They also wanted to reassert their authority on the seas. As a whole, the southern and western states were for war, while the northeastern states were against it. The War of 1812, or what some termed "The Second American Revolution," began later that year.

Huwa says of the conflict, "It was a very unpopular war, but through that very difficult time, Madison stayed true to his constitutional principles; there was no retreating on civil liberties or freedom of speech, or freedom of the press." In 1814, the British marched on the nation's capital, invaded the city of Washington, and burned the White House and other government buildings. Before they arrived, Dolly Madison saved several items from the home, including the Gilbert Stuart portrait of George Washington. "She turned what could have been a public relations disaster into a public relations triumph because of her own bravery," notes Huwa.

In December of 1814, delegates from the New England states met in Hartford to discuss their grievances against the president and the war. There was some talk that those states might even leave the

Union. "The thought of it coming apart [the Union] would not have been that much of a surprise to many people. It was an unpopular war, particularly in New England. There was talk of dissolving the Union and Madison thought that would have been a great disaster," says Huwa. However, soon after the meeting, Andrew Jackson led the Americans to victory in New Orleans and a peace treaty with Britain was signed. With the unexpected end of the war, the meeting in Hartford appeared treasonous, and the delegates' recommendations for changes to the Constitution were dismissed.

Dolly Madison's bravery at the White House is still remembered today, and James Madison's contributions to the Constitution still stand. "I think he would be pleasantly surprised that the basic framework of government that he established exists today," notes Huwa. Together, the president and first lady were a dynamic duo. People of that time realized it as well. Huwa says that one of Madison's presidential challengers was quoted as saying, "If I could have been able to run against just one of them I probably could have won, but against both of them I had no chance."

James and Dolly Madison should still serve as role models today. Of Madison, Huwa explains, "In some ways he was an unlikely hero. He was physically short, he had a weak speaking voice, and he was often sick. Despite all those things he emerged as a leader. All of us have our shortcomings, and Madison overcame many of his to become truly one of the great presidents, the father of the Constitution—maybe we can all draw some lessons from that." Together, James and Dolly Madison show us how individual talents can combine to form a strong and unbeatable dynamic duo.

Seeking Solutions
CHARLOTTESVILLE, VIRGINIA

"You could turn his soul inside out and not find a speck upon it."

—THOMAS JEFFERSON OF JAMES MONROE

Did you know James Monroe . . .

...WAS A NEXT DOOR NEIGHBOR OF THOMAS JEFFERSON?
...WAS PART OF WASHINGTON'S FAMOUS CROSSING OF THE DELAWARE?
...HAS A CAPITAL CITY IN AFRICA NAMED AFTER HIM?

It was Christmas night, 1776. Having faced a string of defeats that demoralized his army, General George Washington was ready to surprise the Hessian defenders of Trenton and hopefully turn his army's fortunes in a positive direction. Under the cover of darkness, he assembled his troops and then ferried the army across the ice-clogged Delaware River. First battling sleet and then snow that began to fall, their fighting force reassembled on the other side and did surprise the Hessian defenders of Trenton, routing them on December 26, 1776.

Just before the main body of Washington's troops crossed the river that Christmas night, an eighteen-year-old named James Monroe and a small group of men rowed ahead to knock out guards who might be watching for an attack. Monroe took a bullet wound to his shoulder, a bullet that remained in his arm the rest of his life. Barking dogs just happened to awaken a doctor who came out to see what was transpiring. That doctor treated Monroe's wound and most likely saved his life. It took him eleven weeks to recover from the injury.

Years later, the future president's role in the important battle was recognized in Emmanuel Leutze's famous painting *Washington Crossing the Delaware* that is seen in many history books today. Although Monroe crossed the icy river long before Washington that night, Americans' lofty opinion of James Monroe led him to be portrayed in a new way in the artist's rendition of the events. "In the commemorative painting, George Washington stands in the front of the boat. Immediately behind him is a younger man holding the American flag and that is James Monroe. This is historically incorrect, but it does show the regard Americans had for these two distinguished patriots," says Carolyn Holmes, executive director of Ash Lawn-Highland, the home of President James Monroe.

After the war, Monroe returned to Virginia to study law under Thomas Jefferson. The two became friends, and Jefferson later persuaded Monroe to move to Charlottesville, Virginia, near his own home of Monticello. James Monroe established his own plantation home now called Ash Lawn-Highland just two miles from Monticello, and the two future presidents' lands shared a common boundary.

Monroe held several political posts in the late 1700s before President Jefferson, in 1803, sent Monroe to France to negotiate safe passage for U.S. ships entering New Orleans. Monroe was fluent in French and had served as minister to that nation under President Washington. Upon Monroe's arrival, he found he could do much more than secure safe passage for ships. Napoleon was willing to sell the entire Louisiana Purchase to the United States! Holmes recounts, "In this case [Monroe] said, 'I'll buy all the land and I give you my personal word of honor it will be paid for.'" Monroe often struggled to make ends meet on his farm and at home, yet he acquired the Louisiana Purchase merely on his word that the U.S. government would pay the bill.

When James Madison became president, Monroe served as his secretary of state, and during the War of 1812 he even led the militia against the British outside of Washington, D.C. He was Madison's successor to the presidency, winning the election of 1816. Monroe began his term with a presidential tour that took him around the country over a span of fifteen weeks. "It was unprecedented, an amount of travel no president before or until quite recently did . . . it was also an opportunity for people to see the president. Very few people had ever laid eyes on a president. He increased that number by thousands and thousands," says Holmes.

During his first term, the Missouri Compromise of 1820 provided a brief solution to the question of slavery, and despite an economic panic in 1819, Monroe's first term was viewed as successful by most Americans. Monroe ran unopposed for re-election in 1820, capturing every electoral vote save one that was cast for John Quincy Adams. During that second term, he developed the Monroe Doctrine, which dictated European countries could no longer attempt to colonize the Americas. That policy is still recognized today as one of Monroe's greatest accomplishments while in office.

Slavery was a thorny issue throughout James Monroe's life. While the Missouri Compromise briefly struck a balance during his presidency, the issue always came back to the forefront. As governor of Virginia in 1800, James Monroe saw slave Gabriel Prosser lead an unsuccessful revolt of one thousand slaves who plotted to seize the arsenal in Richmond, a revolt that the state militia quelled.

Even before Prosser's revolt, other events had shown Monroe just how important it was to resolve the slavery issue. He attended

Virginia's Constitutional Convention in 1788 with a proposal written to free slaves in his state. Holmes says that in conversations at the convention, however, Monroe realized his proposal would have no chance of being ratified.

Though he considered slavery wrong, Monroe feared immediate abolition would result in social and economic upheaval. He became a supporter of colonization, a process whereby slaves would be sent back to Africa to establish a country there. Monroe and Jefferson exchanged ideas on the subject as early as 1800. In 1817, the American Colonization Society was formed and in 1822 established the nation of Liberia on Africa's west coast. Monroe supported the work of the society, and the nation's new capital was named Monrovia in his honor. As a whole the effort failed, although Monroe always seemed to look for diplomatic means to solve the most difficult situations. He once said, "Preparation for war is constant stimulus to suspicion and ill will." Holmes notes, "His ability at diplomacy was outstanding and he helped to solidify the unity of this country."

James Monroe had plenty of experience fighting for his country during the Revolution and the War of 1812. Yet, Monroe always seemed to first seek diplomatic solutions to difficult situations. Jefferson said of him, "You could turn his soul inside out and not find a speck upon it." It was such integrity combined with diplomacy that guided his life. Some historians say Monroe lacked leadership because he always sought to walk a middle ground. Yet, middle ground is exactly where differing sides often must be led to find solutions. Monroe knew that while compromise didn't always work, it was the place to begin, a place to build solutions that would make each person stronger.

The Information Superhighway

QUINCY, MASSACHUSETTS

"Always vote for principle, though you may vote alone, and you may cherish the sweetest reflection that your vote is never lost."

— JOHN QUINCY ADAMS

Did you know John Quincy Adams . . .

. . . TOLD HIS FUTURE WIFE IT MIGHT BE SEVEN YEARS BEFORE HE WOULD COME BACK FOR HER?

. . . WAS THE ONLY PRESIDENT TO SERVE IN THE U.S. HOUSE OF REPRESENTATIVES AFTER HIS TERM AS PRESIDENT?

. . . COULD SPEAK SEVEN DIFFERENT LANGUAGES?

Y ou could call it the information superhighway. Not in terms of Internet connections and computers with the fastest processing speed, but for the late 1700s this highway was its equivalent. This particular information superhighway was a literal highway that ran just ten feet from a young boy's home south of the city of Boston. Old Coast Road was, in fact, one of the most well traveled roads of the day. For a boy named John Quincy Adams, it was this road that provided the latest information of his time, delivering news from one town to another all the way up and down the eastern seaboard.

John Quincy (or "JQA" as he sometimes identified himself) was born on July 11, 1767, a tumultuous time on that road in front of his birthplace. By the time he was old enough to understand his surroundings, the rumblings of a revolution were already quite strong. In the two years immediately before the colonies declared their independence, his father John Adams served as a delegate to the Continental Congress in Philadelphia. The boy often traveled to Boston to collect his father's letters from the mail, and he and his mother learned the latest news from those who would become known as the founding fathers.

Much more than letters traveled that highway, though. "John Quincy Adams would often observe the travelers on the road and hear their stories of what was happening. The militia even practiced maneuvers in his yard, encouraged by his mother Abigail, who was supportive of the War for Independence," says Caroline Kineth, deputy superintendent at the Adam's National Historic Site. John Quincy lived in the reality of war, and he drank in all the events shaping the nation that he would someday oversee as president.

Looking back over two centuries, it is easy to see why the boy would grow up to a life of public service. His youth was a training ground for such a career path. At the age of ten he traveled with his father who was a diplomat in Europe. He learned French in Paris and by the age of fifteen had journeyed through Germany, Russia, and Scandinavia.

Kineth reflects, "His mother, Abigail, had a great influence on his life and believed very strongly that his education should gear him toward serving his country." The two grew quite close while his father, John Adams, was away in Philadelphia. When John and his son departed for Europe, Abigail wrote that the absence of her boy was as if a limb had been cut from her body.

She realized, though, that such a trip was the training a young man would need to serve these colonies turned country. When JQA arrived in France, one of the first letters he received was from his mother, outlining the importance of his time away from home. In it she shared that she would rather him die at sea than be a disgrace to the family and that he should commit himself to the priorities of serving God, country, and family.

As the years passed, JQA did grow into the man his mother had dreamed he would become, an international diplomat schooled in the languages and cultures of Europe. While serving as an ambassador to the Netherlands, he traveled to England in 1795 with one of his friends and there he met a young lady, Louisa Catherine Johnson, the daughter of an American businessman. Kineth relates, "She was a very beautiful girl and was very talented. She spoke French fluently and so did John Quincy Adams. She played the harp and he played the flute. So they had a great deal in common." The couple even put on concerts and plays for their friends and family.

Within a few months JQA went back to the Netherlands, but ideas of marriage were certainly on the horizon. However, the way he went about expressing those feelings seems strange to us today. Kineth says, "He left her with a list of books she should read to improve her mind and with the information that he would see her in one to seven years."

One to seven years! What a way to win someone's heart! It worked, though, and JQA himself must have truly been smitten because he returned at the minimum instead of the maximum time. The two married in 1797, and that same year he was appointed minister to Prussia, a position he served during his father's presidency. This was a time of turmoil for the new bride, as she had to get used to a new country, a new husband, and a new way of life. She had four miscarriages during the time they lived in Prussia.

You may have noticed I've discussed everything here but JQA's term in office. Those four years were not the most successful of his life. He served as secretary of state under James Monroe and then ran for president in 1824. In that contest, no candidate received a majority in the Electoral College and the decision was sent to the House of Representatives. The House selected JQA over Andrew Jackson, a man who had actually received more electoral votes in the election. However, because John Quincy wasn't elected by popular vote or in the Electoral College but by the House of Representatives, he always struggled to gain acceptance as the legitimate candidate to win the White House, and Jackson returned in 1828 to defeat him.

On the other hand, Adams' life after the presidency is as intriguing as his life before the White House. In fact, in front of the U.S. Supreme Court, he successfully defended the Amistad Africans, a group of slaves who seized control of the Spanish ship that was bringing them to America, and the Africans were allowed to return home as free people. He also returned to public service as a member of the U.S. House of Representatives, serving nine consecutive terms in that body. He suffered a stroke on the House floor in February of 1848 and died two days later.

Reflecting on his life and presidency, Kineth says, "John Quincy Adams' policies were ones of great vision for the country. He believed in a national highway system with roads and canals; he wanted to explore the idea of observatories to study the stars. He really had a world beyond himself. He wanted the metric system adopted in the United States."

But the country was not ready to adopt the ideas of John Quincy Adams. Could they have been just too far-reaching for many to embrace? Possibly Adams' upbringing, his extensive travels, and his education had exposed him to ideas most had never dreamed of.

Nonetheless, just imagine what it was like for JQA to make a trip to Europe with his father at such a young age, to experience the diplomatic meetings that influenced the ways governments conducted business. Those experiences began with parents who sought to provide their son with an environment in which he could expand his mind. The learning continued when JQA himself sought knowledge and skills in a variety of countries and institutions, from European halls of government to Harvard Law School to the heavily traveled road in front of his birth home.

Looking back, I see why my father simply "took me along" on trips to town when I was a kid. He may have been looking to buy some farm equipment, visiting with a seed salesman about corn hybrids, or even buying cattle at a local auction. I mostly "just" listened and learned on those trips, but those journeys exposed me to a hands-on learning environment I am grateful for today.

Just like John and Abigail Adams, each of us can provide a nurturing place for our children to learn and grow. We can help them dream great things for their futures. We can also make an effort to educate ourselves and to expose our minds to what we do not know. We can read, listen, travel, and observe what is around us in order to increase our own abilities.

Although President John Quincy Adams is sometimes faulted for not having the confidence of the nation he led, he can be commended for absorbing the information that surrounded him, a quality he learned from his earliest memories while living on, what was then, the information superhighway.

Image Is Everything

"One man with courage makes a majority."

— ANDREW JACKSON

Did you know Andrew Jackson . . .

...MARRIED A LADY WHO WAS TECHNICALLY STILL MARRIED TO
SOMEONE ELSE?

...HAD A PET PARROT THAT SWORE AT HIS FUNERAL?

...KILLED A MAN IN A DUEL?

On the outside, he has to be the roughest and toughest of all presidents. Andrew Jackson was born near Camden, South Carolina, in 1767, two years after his parents emigrated from Ireland. His father died just days before he was born, and he was given the name "Andrew" after his father. His mother and extended family cared for him and even saw that he learned to read, a rare skill in many areas in those days. He probably got his first taste of politics when he was assigned to read newspapers for those who could not do so.

When the Revolutionary War began, he and his brothers joined the cause. His oldest brother died in battle in 1779, and in 1781, Andrew and his brother Robert were captured and taken prisoner after the battle of Hanging Rock. Andrew was only fourteen years old at the time. Both were eventually released in a prisoner exchange, but Robert died of smallpox he contracted while in prison. Their mother later died of cholera when she went to Charleston to help in the war effort. Thus, the Revolution cost Andrew Jackson both of his siblings and his mother.

By 1788, Jackson had become a lawyer and had moved west to the young settlement of Nashville. There he met Rachel Robards, a beautiful young lady known to be a great dancer and a good horsewoman as well. However, Rachel was married to Lewis Robards, and although the two had separated, they were not divorced. The situation proved complicated and a little embarrassing before it was resolved.

Tony Guzzi, curator at Jackson's Nashville home, The Hermitage, says, "Rachel's former husband applied to the state legislature for a divorce, which was the rule at the time, but that divorce never was approved; it had just been applied for. Andrew and Rachel, however, believed the divorce was in fact final and got married. Two years after they wed, they realized the divorce had never been finalized. Rachael's former husband applied for divorce once again, now on the grounds that she was living in sin with another man. So, in a technical sense, Rachael was married to two men at once." Andrew and Rachel quickly remarried once the divorce was final.

In 1802, Jackson became major general of the Tennessee militia and two years later he purchased the farm that he renamed The Hermitage, which would be his and Rachel's home for the rest of their lives, save Jackson's time in the White House. During his days in Nashville, Jackson's image as a rough and tumble character only grew. Guzzi notes, "He wanted to be perceived as this character who didn't take anything off of anyone. It was all a part of his image and it helped him succeed."

In 1803, the governor of Tennessee saw Jackson and made derogatory comments about Rachel. Jackson promptly challenged the governor to a duel, and when he declined, Jackson took out an ad in the newspaper and said the official was a coward. Although that duel never took place, a different one did.

In May of 1806, Charles Dickinson dueled with Jackson. The reason for that contest might also have been comments Dickinson made about Rachel. Dickinson fired first and hit Jackson in the chest, just two inches from his heart. In his book *Andrew Jackson: Portrait of a President,* author Marquis James recounted the event: "A fleck of dust rose from Jackson's coat and his left hand clutched his chest. For an instant he thought himself dying, but, fighting for self-command, slowly he raised his pistol. Dickinson recoiled a step, horror-stricken. 'My God! Have I missed him?' Overton [Jackson's second] presented his pistol. 'Back to the mark, sir!' Dickinson folded his arms. Jackson's spare frame straightened. He aimed . . . and fired. Dickinson swayed to the ground . . . " Dickinson died, but the bullet that hit Jackson didn't kill him, though it remained in his body for the rest of his life.

This was not the only gunfight in Jackson's life. In 1813 Jackson was in a brawl with Jesse and Thomas Hart Benton. In the melee, Jackson was shot in the left arm and all but one doctor recommended amputation. His arm was saved, but he carried the slug until 1832, when it was removed because of discomfort it was causing him. By that time, Thomas Hart Benton had become a senator and friend of Jackson's.

During the War of 1812, Jackson led troops in the south and battled the Creek Indians in 1813. By 1814, he was leading men toward New Orleans to hold back a British invasion there. In December and January of 1815, Jackson won fame as he led his soldiers (a term to be used loosely since the group was composed of volunteers from all over the south and even included Jean Lafitte's band of pirates) to victory over the British.

With national notoriety after his battle in New Orleans and subsequent campaigns in Florida, Jackson ran for president in 1824.

In that race he received more popular and electoral votes than any of the other three candidates, but he did not receive a majority of the votes. Because no candidate received a majority, the election was sent to the House of Representatives as defined in the U.S. Constitution and John Quincy Adams was chosen as president. Jackson returned four years later to defeat Adams.

Jackson's beloved wife Rachel died between the time he was elected and before he took office. He had her grave placed in a nice garden close to the home so that he could visit her often. It was Rachel who had usually calmed the oft-angry Jackson, and friends later noted how much he seemed to miss his wife while he was at the White House.

In 1833, Jackson was riding on a steamboat when he was punched in the nose by a disgruntled military officer. Guzzi says, "That was the first instance of violence against a U.S. president." Two years later he encountered a more serious threat when a would-be assassin approached him after Jackson attended the funeral of a member of the House of Representatives. "He was a housepainter and had become quite deranged and thought he was the descendant to the throne of England and somehow the United States government owed him money and Jackson wasn't paying," explains Guzzi. By assassinating Jackson, he believed someone new would enter the presidency who would look at his claim more favorably. Both pistols misfired when the percussion cap ignited but failed to ignite the powder in the barrel.

Jackson's image was very important throughout his life, including his presidential term. Guzzi continues, "He would bring people into his office and give them that very rough side just to get people to back down from what their position was and come onto his side. He knew that was his public image and he used it to his benefit."

But Jackson was not a frontier bully who tried to intimidate everyone into doing as he wished. In many ways, he had two different sides, a public image that appeared rough and at times mean and angry, while another softer side appeared to those who knew him well. "There's still so much 'What is perception; what is image?' and it's really hard to understand who Jackson really was," explains Guzzi. "Even those who got to know him intimately during his presidential years who had an opinion of him that he was some ruffian from the frontier learned very quickly that his manners were actually very refined and in terms of polite society he held his own."

He not only displayed great love toward his wife, he was also kind toward children. He and Rachel did not have children of their own, but they did adopt one child and cared for several others, including a Creek Indian boy Jackson rescued after one of his battles.

Despite his caring side, it is the "Old Hickory" image of Jackson that most still remember. He was tough and determined, declaring "One man with courage makes a majority." He didn't back down when challenged and sometimes backed up his words with fists or duels. Guzzi correctly asserts, "Jackson in terms of history has been so colored by who he was portrayed in political campaigns that you really do have to be careful when you're looking at him to decide where he really stood." Fittingly, Jackson's tough image was still very present even after his death. At his funeral, his pet parrot had to be removed from the gathering because it was swearing!

Image does color perception, and today Andrew Jackson is usually remembered for his rough and angry nature, while many of his kind and loving actions are never mentioned. Perhaps that's the way he wanted it. Whether we like it or not, image often becomes reality in the minds of those around us and, like Jackson, we should be aware of the image we create through the actions we take.

*"As to the presidency, the two happiest days of my life were
those of my entrance upon the office and my surrender of it."*

—MARTIN VAN BUREN

Did you know Martin Van Buren . . .

...HELPED POPULARIZE THE FAMILIAR PHRASE "O.K."?
...MAY HAVE WORN THE TAIL OF A BUCK DEER ON HIS HAT?
...RAN FOR PRESIDENT ON THE FREE SOIL TICKET?

He was the first president not to be born a British subject.
"Martin Van Buren was born in the last year of the
American Revolution, which was 1782, and he died during the Civil
War in 1862, a very interesting time frame for his life," says Jim
McKay, the chief ranger at Lindenwald, Van Buren's home, and part
of the Martin Van Buren National Historic Site. McKay adds that
Americans know about the Revolution and the Civil War but are
hard pressed to tell you anything that happened in the eighty inter-
vening years, the time frame in which Martin Van Buren lived.

Because few can tell you about that time period in American history, even fewer can tell you much about Martin Van Buren. He was born to parents who owned a tavern in the town of Kinderhook in east central New York. The pub served as a gathering place, regularly hosting political meetings, and that's probably where Van Buren got his first taste of campaigns and elections.

He studied law and passed the bar in 1803 and was elected to the state senate in 1812 as a Democrat-Republican. Determined to defeat the Federalist Party, he even led his own faction of his political party called the "Bucktails," so named because some members wore the tail of a deer on their hat. He quickly became known as an organizer, a man who could rally people behind a common cause. The Bucktails would be one of many rallies he would lead in the political process.

He became New York's attorney general, but was defeated for re-election to that post in 1819, the same year his wife died of tuberculosis. He continued to drum up support for the Democrat-Republicans, and his leadership was rewarded with election to the U.S. Senate in 1821. It was there that he left a lasting impact on national party politics.

While in the Senate, he rallied support for Andrew Jackson and helped him win election in 1828. That year he also won the governor's race in New York, but he only held the post for a few weeks, as Jackson asked him to become his secretary of state. In 1832 he became Jackson's vice president. During the Jackson presidency, the Democratic Party came into existence and Van Buren had a great hand in its development.

McKay says, "Martin Van Buren was one of the founders of the Democratic Party that we have today. He felt that in order for politics to proceed successfully in a nation the size of the United States, you needed to have something for people to rally around." Van Buren was that rally man, helping to develop a political party around which people could focus their support. In fact, Van Buren is given much of the credit for helping develop the two-party political system we have today.

He won the presidency in 1836, but his term suffered from poor timing. The "Panic of 1837" brought a depression that eventually doomed his chances for reelection. Some even dubbed him "Martin Van Ruin" because of the despair most felt. Americans hung the blame for the difficult time on the president, who continued to ride through the streets of the capital in a fine carriage pulled by matching horses attended by uniformed footmen.

Because he was from Kinderhook, New York, the president was sometimes referred to as "Old Kinderhook." In the 1840 election, the nickname was shortened to "O.K." and used in election slogans. New York Democrats even established the "O.K. Club" in support of Van Buren. Most linguists agree that "O.K." actually originated in print in 1839 as slang for "all correct" or in this case a version of "oll korrect." This kept with the fad in the 1830s and '40s of intentionally misspelling phrases and using the resulting initials to refer to them.

It was its frequent use by both political parties in the 1840 election that propelled "O.K." to wide use nationally. One version of the story dispensed by Van Buren's detractors fictitiously assigns the origin of "O.K." to Andrew Jackson. Their assertion was that Andrew Jackson was such a poor speller that he actually spelled "all correct" as "oll korrect." It was really just a tale told to ridicule the Democratic Party to which Jackson and Van Buren belonged.

Whatever the exact origin, Martin Van Buren not only propelled the Democratic Party into existence, he also helped solidify our use of the term "O.K." the world around (although just about no one today could tell you that "O.K." once stood for "Old Kinderhook"). Ironically, the election didn't turn out O.K. for Old Kinderhook, as he lost in the Electoral College 60 to 234. He failed even to carry his home state of New York. Van Buren then ran as a third party candidate on the Free Soil ticket in opposition to the expansion of slavery in 1848, but his ten percent share of the vote did not win him any state.

Van Buren's post presidential years may have been some of the happiest of his life. Of his time in the White House he said, "As to the presidency, the two happiest days of my life were those of my entrance upon the office and my surrender of it." He loved his farm near Kinderhook. It occupied much of his time and he built it into one of the top operations of his era. In fact, McKay points to Van Buren's will as evidence of just how much his home and farming had come to mean to him. "He starts it [his will] off by saying, 'I, Martin Van Buren, of the town of Kinderhook, county of Columbia, state of New York, here to fore governor of the state and more recently president of the United States, but for the last and happiest years of my life a farmer in my native town do make and declare the following to be my last will and testament.'" The document showed just how much he loved his home and working the land.

Although Van Buren's term fell in the midst of a national depression and his life fell in a period often overlooked in American history, the man dubbed "The Little Magician" rallied people behind a cause and made the Democratic Party appear. He realized the importance political parties would play in unifying people's voices behind a cause and candidate. Today we still can learn from Van Buren's example that when we rally behind a cause, we can bring people together to create change.

Keep the Ball Rolling
Charles City, Virginia

"He came back and wrote his inaugural address in the room where he was born and evidently he wrote a bit too long."

—Malcolm "Jamie" Jamieson of
William Henry Harrison

Did you know William Henry Harrison . . .

...Served just one month in office?

...Delivered an inaugural address that spanned nearly two hours?

...Helped popularize the phrase "Keep the ball rolling"?

You might think it difficult to write about a man who served the shortest term in office. It is true that William Henry Harrison was in office but a month before he died, but if you drive to Charles City County, Virginia, to Berkeley Plantation on the banks of the James River, you will find a man who is not only proud of the Harrison family but proud of his own family's lineage on this centuries-old farm.

Malcolm "Jamie" Jamieson shares four centuries of history about the place he calls home. The story began in 1619, when about forty settlers came here on board a ship called the *Margaret*. Jamieson recounts, "At that time they had explicit orders to hold a celebration of Thanksgiving. The Barclay Company . . . was worried about religious discipline, which they thought was lacking in Jamestown." It was recorded in the captain's log that a feast of Thanksgiving to God was held. In fact, Jamieson has a letter from the Kennedy White House verifying this to be the site of the first Thanksgiving, not Plymouth, Massachusetts.

The settlement was vacated in 1622 and sat empty until it was purchased around 1700 by the Harrison family. The home Jameson now owns was built in 1726 by Benjamin Harrison IV. His son, Benjamin Harrison V (the eldest son was always named Benjamin), was a member of the Continental Congress and a signer of the Declaration of Independence. He was also governor of the state of Virginia. It was his second son, William Henry, who went west to fight in the Indian campaigns.

William earned his fame in the Northwest Territories (present day Ohio, Indiana, and Illinois). He defeated the Shawnee chief Tecumseh and his warriors at the battle of Tippecanoe Creek in 1811, earning the nickname "Tippecanoe" in the process, and later defeated the British and their Indian allies in 1813. In that later battle, Tecumseh was killed. A year later Harrison left military life, most likely to satisfy political aspirations now that he had earned fame as a war hero.

For over two decades he bounced from a variety of posts, earning election to Congress and also serving in the Ohio state senate, but he also lost other bids to the U.S. House and Senate and was denied a post as minister to Russia. He also waged an unsuccessful campaign for president in 1836. In 1840, though, he became the Whig nominee for president with John Tyler as his running mate. The two had grown up on plantation farms that were just a few miles from each other along the James River.

In that campaign, Harrison was portrayed as anything but the son of a wealthy and distinguished Virginian family. Jamieson says, "They actually had a campaign picture on a handkerchief that showed him [Harrison] being born in a log cabin, which is a little spin. Actually he was born in this mansion here." His supporters went to great lengths to gain votes for their Whig candidate. One group constructed a ten-foot-wide paper and tin ball with Harrison campaign slogans upon it. They then pushed the ball from town to town, garnering publicity for the presidential contender. Lexicographers believe the event popularized the phrase "Keep the ball rolling."

Harrison did roll to victory in 1840, earning almost four times the electoral votes as incumbent Martin Van Buren. Upon the win, he returned to Berkeley Plantation. "He came back and wrote his inaugural address in the room where he was born and evidently he wrote a bit too long . . . at his inauguration it was a cold wintry day and he stood out for an hour and a half and gave this long speech. He was proud of being a soldier so he didn't wear a hat or heavy coat, and he contracted pneumonia," says Jamieson.

Delivering such long remarks was not that uncommon at the time, but delivering the speech without cover turned deadly. Jamieson says, "They were great on 'speechification' back then. They made these long talks and lack of substance was covered over with the amount of words. They said he fought the whole Indian campaign again out there on the steps of the Capitol." Just thirty-two days after delivering his inaugural address, at the age of sixty-eight, President Harrison died of pneumonia.

That's not nearly the end of the Harrison family story or that of the plantation, though. William Henry Harrison's grandson, Benjamin Harrison, later became the twenty-third president of the United States, and although Benjamin Harrison IX left Berkeley

Plantation when tobacco was no longer profitable, the farm flourishes today under Jamieson's ownership.

During the Civil War, Jamieson said Berkeley was already abandoned and McClellan's northern army camped there. There were 140 gunboats in the river and 140,000 troops encamped on the grounds. President Lincoln even visited to review the troops. While there in July of 1862, General Daniel Butterfield composed "Taps" as a signal for lights out. Butterfield later wrote, "It was three notes and a catch . . . The men would sing, 'Dan, Dan, Dan, Butterfield, Butterfield' to the notes when a call came. Later, in battle or in some trying circumstances or an advance of difficulties, they sometimes sang, 'Damn, Damn, Damn, Butterfield, Butterfield.'"

One of the troops who camped at Berkeley was Mr. Jamieson's grandfather, and when the property came up for sale many years later, his grandfather saw the newspaper ad and purchased the property for the timber. Jamieson recalls, "My father came down here and they [his father and grandfather] camped out. The houses were not habitable, the roofs were falling in, and the windows were all out." The family later restored the home and farm the surrounding land today.

The story of Berkeley Plantation is that of family and tradition. Over a span of four hundred years, it has principally been just two families, the Harrisons and Jamiesons, that have resided here. It is remarkable to see the pride both families have taken in their past and how they continue to share their respective stories. Although William Henry Harrison served but one month as president, it is the story of his home and family that continue to impact visitors today.

Outlaw of Sherwood Forest

"Here lies the body of my good horse, 'The General.'
For twenty years he bore me around the circuit of my
practice, and in all that time he never made a blunder.
Would that his master could say the same!"

—INSCRIPTION ON THE GRAVE
OF JOHN TYLER'S HORSE

Did you know John Tyler . . .

...WAS THE FIRST PRESIDENT TO REMARRY WHILE IN OFFICE?
...SAW MOST OF HIS CABINET RESIGN WITHIN A YEAR?
...WAS EXPELLED FROM HIS POLITICAL PARTY WHILE HE WAS PRESIDENT?

The knock on John Tyler's door at 5:00 a.m. was unexpected, yet the news delivered was not. Tyler had known since before assuming the office of vice president that President William Henry Harrison's health and age might not allow him to live to the end of his four-year term. However, Tyler might never have imagined Harrison's term would cover a mere month.

Yet as that delegation arrived in Williamsburg, Virginia, on the morning of April 5, 1841, no one knew exactly what would or should happen next. Would Tyler become "acting president" and fill out the remainder of the president's four-year term? Would he serve only until a special election was called? Should he retain the title of "vice president" until a decision was reached? John Tyler had the answer.

Edward Crapol, professor of history at the College of William & Mary, says, "He had a little forewarning [of Harrison's poor health] and he acted decisively . . . although perhaps the Constitution was a little fuzzy on this [succession of the vice president], this was something that would add to the stability of the Republic." Tyler insisted that he was the new president and should take the oath of office, serving until the next presidential election in 1844. He did take the oath, fifty-three hours after Harrison passed, and in so doing became the tenth president of the United States.

There were still plenty of people who believed he was not truly president. He had not been elected to his office, and therefore many degraded him by calling him "His Accidency" or addressing him as "Acting President John Tyler." Mail delivered with such a title was returned to the sender unopened. Tyler was determined that he was the president in the same sense every other man had been before him.

For a president who consistently ranks near the bottom of presidential polls, his actions upon taking the office were decisive and very important. He set the precedent that the vice president assumes the office of president if the president should die. Thus, in 1850, when Zachary Taylor died in office, Millard Fillmore became president. A precedent had been set by Tyler and no one questioned what was to happen. It was a process repeated upon the deaths of presidents Lincoln, Garfield, McKinley, Harding, Franklin Roosevelt, and Kennedy. Today the twenty-fifth amendment to the Constitution more clearly defines what is to happen if a vacancy occurs in the office of president or vice president, yet it was Tyler's precedent that stood as the rule for well over a century.

John Tyler retained President Harrison's cabinet, but five months later, all of them resigned save his secretary of state, Daniel Webster. Tyler had vetoed two bills establishing a national bank, and those actions, along with other views that broke from the Whig Party and his cabinet, caused his entire party to reject him. Just days after his cabinet had resigned, the Whigs expelled him from the party and ran national newspaper ads to publicize their action. By 1842 his former party had even brought impeachment charges against him after he vetoed tariff bills. Just a year into his term, John Tyler was a president without a political party and without his original cabinet. To make matters worse, his wife Letitia, who had been bedridden for most of his short term, died in September of 1842.

Soon, though, a young lady, Julia Gardiner, caught the president's eye and the two began to see each other at social events. One such occasion came in February of 1844 when the president, several members of his new cabinet, and other dignitaries were on board the new Navy warship *Princeton*. The vessel was equipped with the largest naval gun in the world, called the Peacemaker. As the party of over three hundred took a cruise on the Potomac, the gun was fired for the guests.

After the demonstration many people went below deck for drinking and singing. Later, there was a request for one more firing of the Peacemaker, but just as President Tyler and Miss Gardiner were to step upstairs, another round of singing began and a friend persuaded them to stay. When the Peacemaker was fired, it exploded, killing Secretary of State Abel Upshur and several others, including David Gardiner, Julia's father. Crapol notes, "I think the trauma of that event attracted her further to John Tyler." He proposed marriage two months later and they were married in 1844.

Julia was thirty years younger than the president, and Tyler's first three children were older than his new bride. Together, Julia and John Tyler had seven children of their own, the last born when John was seventy years old. His fifteen children were born over a span of forty-five years, and despite the fact that John Tyler was born in 1790, some of his grandchildren lived into the 21st century!

Although President Tyler was confronted with many challenges during his term, he did set precedents that are still recognized today. The Tyler Doctrine in 1842 was an extension of the Monroe Doctrine and applied to areas of the Pacific. In 1844 he annexed Texas by a joint resolution of Congress when he knew there might be opposition of such legislation in the Senate. That method of incorporating new lands into the country was used again by President McKinley in 1898 when Hawaii became a U.S. territory. Tyler also sent the first repre-sentative to China in 1844 and established trading relations with that country. As Crapol notes, "I don't find him to be a failure in the broader sense because he set precedents that influenced later presi-dents and influenced the history of the United States."

John Tyler did not run for election in 1844 and he and his family retired to their home on the James River near Charles City, Virginia. Upon arrival there, Tyler gave the place a name he thought fitting. "The story goes that he named it Sherwood Forest after Robin Hood since he [Tyler] would be an [political] outlaw in his own forest," says Crapol. The gravestone of his cherished horse is also on the grounds of that home and gives insight into what Tyler may have thought of his four years in office. It reads, "Here lies the body of my good horse, 'The General.' For twenty years he bore me around the circuit of my practice, and in all that time he never made a blunder. Would that his master could say the same!"

The political outlaw of the nation chaired a "Peace Convention" in 1861 to attempt to avert a Civil War. When that failed he voted with his state of Virginia for secession and was elected to the Confederate House of Representatives. He died in January of 1862, just before that body met. When he died, he was no longer a citizen of the United States but instead a citizen of the Confederacy.

Although Tyler's challenges in office and his vote to secede from the Union often make him a less than popular president, the impact of some of Tyler's decisions are still felt today. When the presidency was in question, Tyler was decisive and took the oath of office as the tenth chief executive. His annexation of Texas and the opening of relations with China were also decisions that positively influenced the country.

Precedents are important in life. They establish an example to be followed by others. Although he may not have realized it at the time, when John Tyler took the oath of office as president, he set one of the most important precedents surrounding the presidency itself. His decisive action resulted in a smooth exchange of power when the situation arose again.

Our actions are very important because they not only affect the present, they form an example to be followed in the future. Certainly precedents may be later altered, yet the power of what is done in the beginning carries great weight. Those decisions form the traditions followed in our families, communities, businesses, and the world.

Go West, Young Man
COLUMBIA, TENNESSEE

*"No president who performs his duties faithfully and
conscientiously can have any leisure."*

—JAMES K. POLK

Did you know James K. Polk . . .

...AS A YOUNG MAN HAD TO TRAVEL OVER TWO HUNDRED MILES FOR
A LIFE-SAVING SURGERY?

...EXPANDED THE SIZE OF THE NATION BY OVER 800,000 SQUARE MILES?

...RECEIVED A BURIAL AT THREE DIFFERENT LOCATIONS?

A s a young boy, James K. Polk always seemed to live on the
western edge of an ever-growing country. Fittingly, the
youngster who would grow to manhood on the frontier would do
much to push this nation westward, literally moving the boundary of
the United States to the Pacific Ocean.

Today much of that story is told at the Polk Ancestral Home in
Columbia, Tennessee, a small city set among rolling country hills in the
central section of the Volunteer State. Although it's not the location

where James Polk began or ended his life, it's a city in which he grew to learn the lessons that would propel him to political success. John Holtzapple is the director of that home, a two-story family dwelling that attracts presidential enthusiasts and visitors who venture down from the country music capital of Nashville.

As we strolled through the home, Holtzapple spoke of the Polk family's constant push to the frontier. "The westward expansion went with James K. Polk's upbringing. If you trace the Polk family from when they came to North America, generation to generation they moved west. They initially settled on the eastern shore of Maryland. The next generation moved northwest into Pennsylvania and the next generation traveled southwest into North Carolina. Polk's father and grandfather moved into Tennessee, and James Polk in his lifetime saw some of his cousins and distant relatives push into Arkansas and Texas."

James Polk was born in 1795 near Charlotte, North Carolina, a place considered to be "the west" at the time. But his father, a farmer and land surveyor, was always looking to move further into the wilderness, and the family moved to Tennessee when James was just ten. Eventually the family would settle near the town of Columbia, Tennessee.

It is hard to imagine Columbia as a western town, but when the Polks lived there it represented life on the frontier. Shortly before his seventeenth birthday, James needed surgery to remove stones from his urinary bladder. Because the family lived so far from the rest of the country's population, finding a doctor who could perform the surgery proved difficult. They traveled 230 miles to Kentucky where noted surgeon Ephraim McDowell performed the operation. The situation proved how isolated the family was from the rest of the nation.

Young James studied law and rode a circuit of courts in his area and went on to win a seat in the state legislature at the age of only twenty-seven. He moved on to the U.S. House of Representatives and even served as Speaker of the House from 1835-1839. He then returned to his home state of Tennessee where he was governor until 1841.

When the Democrats held their party's nominating convention in Baltimore, Maryland, in the summer of 1844, the delegates deadlocked between former president Martin Van Buren and Lewis Cass, a former minister to France and Andrew Jackson's secretary of war. Neither could get the required votes to secure their place on the ballot. When Democrats finally saw that the effort to select either one of the men was fruitless, Van Buren put his support behind the country's first true dark horse presidential candidate. Thus, James K. Polk became the presidential contender even though he wasn't even present at the party's convention.

The Polk Ancestral Home is the last remaining structure outside of the White House in which Polk lived. It was here that Polk lived between his college graduation in 1818 and his marriage in 1824. Holtzapple explains that although Polk was a dark horse, the presidential contender quickly assembled an impressive list of goals he was determined to accomplish. "Expansion in the southwest to California, the annexation of the Oregon Territory in the northwest, establishing an independent treasury department, and lowering tariffs," were some of the major goals Polk set for his tenure in office. What's more, Polk said he would accomplish these ambitious goals in only four years, since he desired to serve only one term as president.

James K. Polk was a president consumed with the work of governing the nation, a very hands-on man who looked after every detail of the office. "Only three times during his term in office did he travel more than a day's trip away from Washington. He hated to be out of touch," says Holtzapple. It was indicative of how Polk viewed the presidency. He once remarked, "No president who performs his duties faithfully and conscientiously can have any leisure."

But his hardworking attitude did not cause him to forget that he was first and foremost a servant of the people. Holtzapple explains, "He opened his White House office to anyone who wanted to see [him]. On weekdays from around nine in the morning until noon, anyone who wanted to see the president could come and see the president." Travelers brought their children to meet President Polk, and there were a great number of job seekers who showed up, too, a dilemma that sometimes frustrated him.

Polk made good on the goals he set upon entering the White House. Negotiations with Great Britain acquired the Oregon Territory for the U.S. in 1846 and the two-year-long Mexican War resulted in the addition of much of the present day southwestern U.S., including portions of Nevada, Utah, Wyoming, New Mexico, Arizona, and California. Over 800,000 square miles of territory were added to the nation during his presidency.

Polk epitomized "Manifest Destiny," a view that the United States should and would grow to a nation that spanned a continent. It must have frustrated him when others lacked his expansionist dream. Polk could have felt that his own successor, Zachary Taylor, lacked that vision. Holtzapple relates, "Zachary Taylor, on the ride to his inauguration, said to the effect, 'Maybe it's good that we have Oregon and California as a U.S. territory,' but Taylor never thought Oregon or California would become states because they were so far away. That really disturbed Polk. From his point of view, the United States didn't acquire all that land just to sit vacant." Of course, those lands began to fill when events like the discovery of gold in California sent thousands rushing to the other side of the country.

Polk's hardworking, goal-oriented demeanor should be tempered with his view of the presidency as a servant leadership position, a role he commented on several times. He wrote in his diary shortly before leaving the White House, "I will soon cease to be a servant and become a sovereign." Holtzapple adds, "His full political career he was a servant of the people, but now he was going to become an average citizen and that would give him the power."

James and Sarah Polk moved to a large home in Nashville when his term was complete, but the president never got to enjoy much time as an average citizen. Only three months after returning to his home state he contracted cholera and died at the age of 53. Because of regulations regarding cholera deaths, Polk had to be buried immediately outside of the Nashville city limits. That first burial took place with little of the ceremony normally bequeathed to a president who has passed. Once the epidemic subsided, he was reinterred on the grounds of his Nashville home.

Sarah lived for forty-two years after her husband's death and never remarried. Upon her death, the president's body, buried at that Nashville home site, was exhumed once again and he was buried for a third time, this time next to his wife, on the grounds of the state capitol.

Historians often praise Polk for the amount of work he accomplished in only one term. He set clearly defined goals and went out and achieved them. His hands-on, persistent approach was meant to generate results. That determination was not lost on the people of Polk's era. Holtzapple says, "Certainly his diligence . . . his dedication to the job, his belief he was serving others by doing this job . . . I think those are qualities Polk's own contemporaries admired, whether they agreed with his policies or not."

Polk should also be admired for his desire to serve the people. He never lost sight of that, as evidenced through his words and actions. He enjoyed visiting with the people he governed. They were his boss, and he invited them into his office to share what was on their minds or simply to bring their children by to visit. These are lessons we learn from a "frontier" president who helped push his country's boundaries to the other side of the continent.

President for a Day?

Plattsburg, Missouri

"The judge waked me up at three o'clock in the morning and said jocularly that I was president of the United States and he wanted me to appoint him as secretary of state."

—David Rice Atchison

Did you know David Rice Atchison . . .

...May have served as president for a day?
...Had a county, city, and railroad named for him?
...Slept through most of his "term" in office?

I n front of the Clinton County courthouse in Plattsburg, Missouri, there is a statue of one of the leading political figures of the mid-nineteenth century. His name is David Rice Atchison, and although the statue of the prominent legislator is placed at the front entrance of the building for all to see, it is the plaque on the monument that may be the most unique in presidential history.

According to Helen Russell, an authority on the life of Atchison, a political figure with plenty of ties to northwest Missouri, "He was very well known, very well respected and loved by those who knew him." Russell recounts that Atchison was instrumental as a state legislator in helping Missouri acquire the Platte Purchase. That land today forms the six counties in the northwestern "neck" of the Show-Me State. In fact, Missouri's northwestern-most county is named Atchison County in honor of the politician.

Atchison was born August 11, 1807, in Frogtown, Kentucky. A bright young man, he attended Transylvania College (later incorporated into the University of Kentucky) when he was only fourteen, where he was a classmate of the future president of the Confederacy, Jefferson Davis. By 1830 he had moved to western Missouri to practice law, and four years after that he was in the Missouri state legislature.

It was his appointment by the governor in 1842 to fill the unexpired term of one of the state's senators that propelled him to national importance. He remained in the Senate until 1855, eventually being elected president of the body. As President Pro Tem of the Senate, Atchison was a national leader whose opinion was very important in shaping national legislation.

Despite his many accomplishments, it is one particular day of Atchison's life for which most will always remember him . . . March 4, 1849. "It fell on a Saturday night when Polk's term expired and the new president [Taylor] who had been elected refused to take office on Sunday," says Russell.

Therein lay the problem. Who was president? Polk's term by law had ended but Taylor's term had not yet begun since he had refused to take the oath of office on a Sunday. Normally the vice president of the United States would fill this role, but vice president George Dallas' term had expired at the same time as that of his boss, President Polk. By law, the presidency then fell to the President Pro Tem of the Senate, David Rice Atchison.

Historians debate whether Atchison actually was in charge of the country for that one day between the Polk and Taylor presidencies.

Russell explains, "He's in the congressional record as being president for that day; at least it's mentioned in one place. But other people still deny that he was president for a day." Some say he should not be considered president since he never took the oath of office. Others counter by asking, "Who then was president?"

Possibly more interesting was whether or not Atchison himself believed he was president and what he did during his one-day term. An 1882 article in the Plattsburg, Missouri, newspaper, *The Lever,* recounted an interview with Senator Atchison in which he was asked the circumstances by which he became president for a day.

Atchison replied, "It was in this way: Polk went out of office on the third of March 1849, on Saturday at twelve noon. The next day, the fourth, occurring on Sunday, General Taylor was not inaugurated. He was not inaugurated until Monday the fifth, at twelve noon. It was then canvassed among senators whether there was an interregnum (which means a time during which a country lacks a government). It was plain that there was either an interregnum or I was the President of the United States, being chairman of the Senate, having succeeded Judge Magnum of North Carolina. The judge waked me up at three o'clock in the morning and said jocularly that I was President of the United States and he wanted me to appoint him as secretary of state. I made no pretense to the office, but if I was entitled in it I had one boast to make, that not a woman or a child shed a tear on account of my removing any one from office during my incumbency of the place."

Atchison was known for his humor, and Russell says, "It was just kind of a fluke that he made light of. He joked about it, but I don't think he ever considered himself to be president." Atchison did say that he slept through most of his term, having spent several long days working in the Senate the previous week.

Although it is a unique honor to have possibly been president of the United States for one day, it actually may be a great injustice to

Atchison. Russell explains, "I would like for him to be remembered for things a lot more important than what he did that one day." History seems to have overlooked the accomplishments of David Rice Atchison and instead makes light of him as a hapless man in charge of the country. "I think it's been an injustice to him that he is just remembered as being president for a day when he did so many other great things." He had a twelve-year career in the U.S. Senate besides serving as a representative in the Missouri legislature. Numerous locations and businesses are named for him, including Atchison County, Missouri, the city of Atchison, Kansas, and the Atchison, Topeka, and Santa Fe railway.

It is unfortunate that some men and women are only remembered for one, or just a few, "events" in their lives. In today's fast-paced world, we sometimes tend to quickly label people instead of taking the time to appreciate their unique qualities and accomplishments. All too often, these individuals can never shake such labels, no matter what they do, and we miss out on the wonderful qualities they truly possess.

To merely tag Atchison with the title "President for a Day" is to miss out on his many other actions that shaped the state of Missouri and the nation during the mid 1800s. The debate over whether or not Atchison was president for a day may never be settled, but as for the plaque on the monument in front of the Clinton County Courthouse in Plattsburg, it proclaims Atchison was indeed "President for a Day." However, for Helen Russell and others in northwest Missouri, he is appropriately remembered for much, much more.

Old Rough and Ready

LOUISVILLE, KENTUCKY

"For more than half a century, during which kingdoms and empires have fallen, this Union has stood unshaken. The patriots who formed it have long since descended to the grave; yet still it remains, the proudest monument to their memory . . . "

—ZACHARY TAYLOR

Did you know Zachary Taylor . . .

...NEVER RAN FOR A POLITICAL OFFICE BEFORE WINNING THE PRESIDENCY?

...WAS SOMETIMES MISTAKEN FOR A FARMER WHILE HE WAS A GENERAL?

...WAS THE SUBJECT OF A MURDER INVESTIGATION 141 YEARS AFTER HIS DEATH?

He had the lineage of a president, but for much of his life he didn't look the part. Zachary Taylor was a man whose family tree included James Madison (a second cousin), Robert E. Lee, and the pilgrims on the Mayflower. Yet, as a boy growing up on a farm just outside of Louisville, Kentucky, Taylor's methods were often far nearer to a man who worked the land than a person leading a nation.

James Holmberg, curator of special collections at the Filson Historical Society in Louisville, the city Taylor considered his hometown for much of his early life, notes, "He was a homespun kind of guy . . . if he hadn't been a soldier he would have been a farmer." But a soldier he was, a very good one in fact, who would someday become a national hero of the Mexican War.

Although the state of Virginia claims him as one of "their" presidents, Zachary Taylor's family moved to Kentucky when he was only one year old. He grew up on his parent's farm and later joined the military as a young adult. It was Taylor's leadership on the battlefield that propelled him to national fame, yet it was his agricultural roots that always seemed to show through.

"One of the things many people noted is that he looked like a farmer. He didn't wear his uniform or maybe only part of it. He'd go around with a duster on or maybe a straw hat. They said he always looked more like a country gentleman than he did a general in the United States Army," says Holmberg. In fact, new men assigned to Taylor's post might bump into him and not even realize they were speaking with their commander. He would ask them what they had heard about "the old general," only to reveal his true identity later, much to the newcomer's chagrin.

It was during the Seminole wars that Taylor earned the nickname "Old Rough and Ready," a moniker that would stick with him the rest of his life. His reputation as a determined leader on the battlefield also stuck and helped him advance to higher ranks. By 1845 he was in command of a small army in southern Texas. The next year, when the Mexican War began, Taylor's troops were victorious in battle, sometimes defeating armies larger than their own.

Taylor's most famous battle came in February of 1847 at the Battle of Buena Vista. There he was outnumbered by Santa Anna four to one yet he led his troops to victory. Holmberg reflects, "He often led by example right there in the thick of things. His men loved him. You can't just be lucky that long . . . he had to be a talented soldier."

By the end of the Mexican War, Taylor had become so popular that he was nominated by the Whig Party for president and won the election of 1848, despite the fact that he had never voted in a presidential election before that time. (This was mostly due to his constant travels in the army, which made it difficult to establish residency to vote.)

Curiously, while Taylor was a slaveholder himself, his policies sought to limit the expansion of slavery. Debate raged in Congress, and it appeared the country might split in two. Holmberg says, "Some people think he was politically naive because he didn't play the political game real well, but he wasn't interested in playing the political game." Taylor was determined to keep the states together, and he stated, "For more than half a century, during which kingdoms and empires have fallen, this Union has stood unshaken. The patriots who formed it have long since descended to the grave; yet still it remains, the proudest monument to their memory . . . "

We'll never know how Taylor's policies on slavery might have affected the country. After a Fourth of July celebration in 1850 at the Washington Monument, Taylor drank iced milk and ate cherries on the way back to the White House. He was dressed in a high collared black suit and may have been suffering from heat stroke. The cold milk and cherries were a shock to his system. By the time he returned to the presidential home, he had developed severe stomach pains. The inflammation of his stomach and intestines, a condition called cholera morbus, resulted in his death on July 9, just five days later.

141 years later, a theory was advanced that Taylor might have been poisoned by political rivals. His symptoms at the time of death were consistent with arsenic poisoning and his body was consequently

exhumed in 1991 to see if he had been murdered. Samples of hair and fingernails were examined at Oak Ridge National Laboratory, but no signs of elevated arsenic levels were found.

Considering that Taylor's first elected office was that of president of the United States, it makes sense that he may have lacked the political experience that would have proved helpful in his presidential term. "He may not have been as effective and talented a politician as many other presidents we've had, but I think in his mind he was doing what he thought was right, despite what the political consequences might have been," says Holmberg.

As both general and president, Taylor offered a "common man" approach to life. Speaker of the House Robert Winthrop recalled the president elect's unfamiliarity with Washington politics before his inaugural ceremony. Winthrop stated that he was "much impressed by [Taylor's] simplicity of character." It wasn't meant as a put-down, but rather a compliment to a man who never "put on airs."

"Simplicity of character" does not mean simplicity of mind. It is rather an approach to life that helped Taylor focus on the people and things most important to him. It's a view Taylor used as general and president to relate to those he led, to help them feel comfortable around him. It's an idea we can apply in life as well.

Oswego
Boonville
Youngstown Newfane Lockport Greece Rochester Fulton Camden Rome
agara Falls Brighton Newark Liverpool Oneida Utica Sarat
Tonawanda Buffalo Cheektowaga Canandaigua Auburn Syracuse Morrisville Fort Plain Canaj
West Seneca Geneva
Erie Hamburg Angola Springville Yah Lansing Oneonta
Dunkirk Cooperstown
Fredonia Alfred Corning Sidney Delhi
Westfield Gang Mills Johnson City Walton
Jamestown Olean Wellsville Elmira Binghamton
ULSTER

A Know Nothing?

EAST AURORA, NEW YORK

> "May God save the country, for it is evident
> that the people will not."
>
> —MILLARD FILLMORE

Did you know Millard Fillmore . . .

...MARRIED HIS TEACHER?

...RAN FOR PRESIDENT ON THE KNOW NOTHING PARTY'S TICKET?

...KEPT THE NATION FROM CIVIL WAR FOR ANOTHER DECADE?

The great thing about visiting presidential sites is the dedicated people you meet who share the story of "their" president. Often, at smaller sites, these are people who volunteer their time to open the homes and historic sites and share the stories of presidential families. Marie Schnurr is one such individual, a long-time resident of East Aurora, New York, just outside of Buffalo, who enjoys sharing the story of "her" president, Millard Fillmore.

But on my first trip to Buffalo, even Marie's dedicated presidential spirit was tested when a storm dumped its usual winter blanket on the area and the small Fillmore homestead was reduced to something more akin to an igloo than a presidential site. After a quick phone call, we both decided that shoveling that much snow to do an interview about Millard Fillmore just wasn't worth it. But when I parked my rental car in front of the home three months later on a return trip to the area, I now found a home whose winter snow had melted into a springtime backdrop of flowers and budding trees.

Millard was the second of nine children, born in 1800 in western New York. The location of the family's farm meant this family's children would get little formal schooling. "There was a wilderness here," Marie said as we pulled up a chair around the Fillmore's dining table. "There were no homes close by. The only time there was any school for the kids was when an itinerant teacher might pass through."

What formal schooling Fillmore did receive proved to be valuable in more ways than one. In 1819 he enrolled in an academy in New Hope, New York, where he found a teacher who would inspire him to learn. Her name was Abigail Powers, and Marie notes, "In the evenings he went to her school and she did help further his education," even inspiring him to study law and pass the bar. But the eighteen-year-old Fillmore also fell in love while attending that school and a relationship developed between the teacher, less than two years his senior, and the student. The two married in 1826.

Millard built this small dwelling just before he and Abigail wed and the two lived here for the first five years of their marriage. It is this home that remains today . . . a home in which Marie tells the story of a president about whom few know many details. His rise to the presidency included service in the state legislature and the U.S. House of Representatives. He was later selected to run on war hero Zachary Taylor's Whig Party ticket as his vice presidential candidate. The two won the election of 1848, but just over halfway through his term, Taylor died in office and Fillmore assumed the presidency.

The two decades before the American Civil War proved to be difficult times for any man holding the office. Each tried to preserve a nation that was headed for secession and war. Fillmore signed the Compromise of 1850, a measure unpopular in the north because it contained the fugitive slave law that imposed heavy fines for anyone aiding slaves to attain their freedom. Southerners also disliked the law because it admitted California to the union as a free state and prohibited the slave trade in the District of Columbia. Fillmore saw it as a way to keep the Union together, though he may have believed that task to be ultimately futile. Fillmore stated, "May God save the country, for it is evident that the people will not."

"God knows that I detest slavery, but it is an existing evil, for which we are not responsible, and we must endure it, till we can get rid of it without destroying the last hope of free government in the world," said Fillmore. The compromise avoided war for another decade, but Fillmore's support of the law made the Whigs choose Winfield Scott to run for president instead of him in 1852.

Fillmore returned to run for president in 1856 as part of the Know Nothing Party, a group that earned the nickname because their members often responded to questions about their views with a simple "I don't know" instead of a lengthy explanation of their stance. In reality the group was opposed to Roman Catholics and immigrants and avoided taking a firm stand on the issue of slavery. Marie says, "It wasn't so much that Millard Fillmore supported their platform, but he did want to run for president again and they ran him." With the desire to run and an upstart party looking for a big-name candidate, Fillmore entered the race. The former president carried but one state, Maryland.

His teacher and wife, Abigail, died just after he left the presidency in 1853. Sadly, she died of pneumonia after attending the chilly inauguration of her husband's successor, Franklin Pierce.

Fillmore remarried and returned to Buffalo, where he set out to accomplish much for his home community.

His return to western New York still impacts the area today. Marie rattles off a list that seems to go on and on of what Millard Fillmore accomplished after his time in the Oval Office and his stint as a "Know Nothing." "He was the first chancellor of the University of Buffalo, he was one of the founders of Buffalo General Hospital, a founder of the Buffalo Historical Society and its first president, he founded the Buffalo Club for professional men, he was on the board of the museum of science and the art gallery, and he gave books for the beginning of the Buffalo Public Library," says Marie.

Marie adds that Americans today should remember Fillmore for his local leadership and community service. "He was very active until the day of his death at age seventy-eight. Up until that time he was always involved in the city of Buffalo. There was always some cause that he was interested in and tried to further."

The legacy Fillmore left on his hometown can be seen in much more than East Aurora's Fillmore Avenue and Buffalo's Fillmore Street. The impact runs deeper than mere street signs, for it is a legacy that continues to help the people of the area through the organizations and institutions he helped establish.

What's refreshing is that this "favorite son" didn't forget his home. He returned to make a difference in people's lives, devoting himself to aiding others. While few can tell you much about a "Know Nothing" from western New York, they can quickly tell you about a man who "Did Something" for his hometown. It was Millard Fillmore who worked to create positive change in his community, an example that still stands today.

*"You have summoned me in my weakness.
You must sustain me by your strength."*

—FRANKLIN PIERCE

Did you know Franklin Pierce's . . .

...VICE PRESIDENT WAS SWORN INTO OFFICE IN CUBA?

...INAUGURAL ADDRESS STATED THAT HE DID NOT DESIRE TO BE
PRESIDENT?

...CABINET INCLUDED THE FUTURE PRESIDENT OF THE CONFEDERACY?

As he entered his term as president, Franklin Pierce's short biography might have read this way: "Very handsome, a people person who is great with names, friendly and popular, from a politically well-connected family in New England. A friend to Catholics and the youngest president to be elected, whose major task is to make peace between two enemies on the brink of war." It is a description most people would attribute to John F. Kennedy, but the paragraph could be used to describe the man who entered the presidency over a century before JFK, the fourteenth president of the United States, Franklin Pierce.

However, the similarities diverge from that inauguration day snapshot, making the title "The First JFK" truly a misnomer. What the two presidents would accomplish and how they would deal with conflict during their terms quickly sets the two apart. Unlike Kennedy, who is still quoted extensively and is regarded as a great president whose term was cut short by an assassin, Pierce's presidency is often lost among a string of one-termers leading up to Abraham Lincoln.

The Pierce Manse, the home of the former president from 1842 to 1848, is in Concord, New Hampshire. Florence "Chips" Holden, the president of the Pierce Brigade, a group that restored the home, retells the story of how this young man emerged as a candidate and victor in the presidential race of 1852.

"He didn't have any intention of running for president," Chips explains. Nominated on the forty-eighth ballot on a sweltering day in Baltimore, it may have been a case where the scorched delegates simply wanted to end the process and just put any man's name on the ballot so they could go home.

With tensions escalating ahead of the Civil War, a conflict that would break out in less than a decade, both the Democratic and Whig parties were looking for a candidate who would not be controversial. Normally, political parties would be looking for a strong statesman with bold leadership skills, but in the political climate of the 1850s the reverse was true. Any man with strong opinions either for or against slavery would alienate a large segment of the voters, and because many of the leading candidates had already taken strong stands on the issue, they stood little chance of securing the votes needed to win their party's nomination. In the end, the Democrats selected a northerner who was a supporter of state's rights. That man was Franklin Pierce.

The fact that the Democrats were looking for someone who was reserved in his political prowess is not to infer that Pierce was an unworthy candidate. He had early and lofty success in politics. By the age of twenty-four he was already a representative in the New Hampshire legislature and two years later he became the speaker of that body. He had also served as a representative and senator in the U.S. Congress, not to mention that he was a successful and well-known lawyer in his native Granite State.

"He was a great peacemaker and that's what he tried to do before the Civil War. This is what got him in trouble . . . He appeared to be playing both sides," notes Chips. Bringing people together was always his mission, but his efforts often only seemed to make people angry. When the Catholic Church received a cool reception upon its expansion to Concord, it was Pierce who went to the priest and formed a friendship. He befriended the Shakers as well, even though they received an equally chilly welcome to the community. Pierce even provided free legal advice to them as a lawyer before he became president.

Some of Pierce's fiercest opposition in his run for president came from his wife. "She was terribly against it. She had no use for politics. When she got word he had been nominated, she fainted," Chips explains. The husband and wife truly were opposites, with Franklin an outgoing and gregarious man coupled with a shy and reserved wife. It was Jane Pierce's distaste for Washington D.C. and political life that probably pushed Franklin to leave Congress ten years earlier.

If the Democratic party lacked direction in selecting a candidate, the Whig party outdid them in the number of ballots it took to select their own candidate. It took fifty-three tries for the Whigs to select Pierce's Mexican War commander, General Winfield Scott, as their candidate for president. Scott was known for his long and boring speeches and probably did more to lose the election than Pierce did to win it. His nickname, "Old Fuss and Feathers," has to be one of the best in political history.

Upon winning the presidency, Pierce encountered a series of tragedies out of his control that were so depressing they affected his entire term. In January of 1853, two months before being sworn into office, the Pierce family was traveling by train back to their home in New Hampshire when their train derailed and the family's car was thrown from the track. In the accident, the Pierce's only surviving child, Benny, was crushed and killed before his parents' eyes. He was only eleven years old. Two other children had already passed, one in infancy, the other of typhus at the age of four.

Chips says, "Jane always felt this had been a punishment from God for his interest in politics, especially the presidency." For about two years she did not receive any guests at the White House save Jefferson Davis, Nathaniel Hawthorne, and their wives. One of Jane Pierce's cousins served as the hostess for Franklin during most of his term.

Franklin felt the deep despair of his child's death as he entered the presidency. Upon inauguration, he stated, "It is a relief to feel that no heart but my own can know the personal regret and bitter sorrow over which I have been borne to a position so suitable for others rather than desirable for myself." He continued, "You have summoned me in my weakness. You must sustain me by your strength."

Pierce also entered the presidency with a vice president, Rufus King, who was seriously ill. King traveled to Cuba before the inauguration to seek relief from tuberculosis, and by a special act of Congress was allowed to be sworn into office on the island. He died only one month into his term.

With all of his children gone, a wife so depressed she was a recluse, and without a vice president, Pierce probably had more personal tragedy on his mind than any president before him. His peacemaking nature would, ironically, bring domestic troubles as well.

The Missouri Compromise, adopted in 1820, banned slavery in new territories. However, Pierce supported the Kansas-Nebraska Act that would allow those new states to vote for themselves whether they would allow slavery. When Pierce signed the new act into law, fighting broke out as both sides rushed in to provide the votes needed to secure their cause. The term "bleeding Kansas" is used to refer to the bloodshed that occurred during that tumultuous effort to win the vote. Pierce did not send in federal troops to put down the Midwestern war, and many citizens subsequently saw the president as weak and indecisive.

Chips reflects, "If he'd been a strong abolitionist or a strong state slave righter he would have been more popular, but he wasn't. Particularly his friendships with people like Jefferson Davis did not sit well with people in New Hampshire." Davis, who would later become president of the Confederacy, served in Pierce's cabinet as secretary of war. Of course, if Pierce had taken a strong stance on the slavery issue before his election, he never would have been selected as a candidate for the office.

"He came home very unpopular. He had been the most popular man in the country when he became president, and when he came home nobody even met him at the train station," explains Chips. His wife was still depressed, and Pierce took Jane to Europe for three years, hoping the time away would help, but the journey seemed to do little to ease her pain. They eventually returned to Concord and Pierce resumed his law practice.

In the 1860s, when Pierce did not praise Lincoln for his Civil War policies, the people of Concord even marched on his home in angry protest. "The tragedy is that his relationship with everybody was so good, and when it started to fail it went down fast," says Chips. In some ways, Pierce's efforts to be a friend to everyone left him with few friends in the end. The country was not yet ready for a peacemaker. War had to occur first.

In spite of all this, Pierce is to be admired for some of his under-appreciated qualities. His law practice flourished because people trusted him. That was a constant virtue in Pierce's life. Although citizens may have criticized him for his friendships with people they considered to be the enemy, Pierce was genuine and worked hard for the rights of all people, regardless of their views.

In the end, it was Pierce's yearning to bring sides together that caused his presidency to come apart. Personal tragedies also heaped more weight upon already strenuous political situations. Put Pierce and his peacemaking in another period of American history, and he might have been one of the most popular of presidents.

Today Americans can admire Franklin Pierce for his undying efforts to promote peace. He reached out to those in his home state who were deemed unpopular and unfit to live there. He reached out to the south and even put the future president of the Confederacy in his presidential cabinet in hopes of bringing sides together.

As Chips notes, because Pierce was a great peacemaker, people thought he was playing both sides. Certainly difficult times call for each of us to take a stand for what is right. In such times, a person may have to sacrifice personal ties to do this. Yet Pierce can be admired for what so many of us fail to do. He reached out and offered peace to others in his community when so many simply hurled insults and didn't make an effort to communicate. He sincerely wanted to bring sides together, and even though he failed to mend the North and South, probably no person could have done that prior to the Civil War. Each of us has a duty to make an effort to understand others and to work to bring about peaceful solutions. Pierce provides an example from which to learn.

*"If you are as happy, my dear sir, on entering this house
as I am in leaving it and returning home,
you are the happiest man in this country."*

—JAMES BUCHANAN TO ABRAHAM LINCOLN

Did you know James Buchanan . . .

...WAS THE ONLY PRESIDENT NEVER TO MARRY?

...SAW THE CONFEDERATE ARMY ADVANCE TO WITHIN A FEW MILES
OF HIS NORTHERN HOME?

...WAS ALMOST KICKED OUT OF COLLEGE?

H e was the only president never to marry, yet his life speaks of
love . . . love for country, love for the Constitution, and love
for a woman to whom he was engaged.

James Buchanan was born near Mercersburg, Pennsylvania, on
April 23, 1791. The son of a trading post owner, he received his education on the frontier of the Keystone State. He had a knack for debate
and the brains to back up his arguments. But when he went to college,
the skills that would help him in politics almost got him kicked out.

Sam Slaymaker, executive director of the James Buchanan Foundation at Buchanan's home, says, "Buchanan was a good student at Dickinson [College], but he did like to party a bit and was prone to challenging his professors and wasn't sufficiently respectful of them." One summer his father received a letter from the college stating that James was no longer welcome to attend classes there. His father was furious, along with his son, but James said he would change his ways if he were allowed to return. Strings were pulled and Buchanan did go back to Dickinson, even graduating from there.

In 1819 he was engaged to a young lady named Ann Coleman, the daughter of one of the wealthiest men in the country. Her father, Robert Coleman, had made his fortune in the iron business and may have thought Buchanan, a young enterprising lawyer and state legislator, was dating his daughter for the wrong reasons, namely her money. The rift between the Coleman family and Ann and James came to a head, and although the exact details are not known, the couple broke off the engagement and Ann traveled to Philadelphia to be with her sister shortly thereafter. She had been in the city only a week when she suddenly died. Some believe her death may have been a suicide.

Buchanan was heartbroken over the loss. The Coleman family would not allow him to attend the funeral and many believed it was Buchanan who was to blame for the sad turn of events. Although the future president never spoke of the impact Ann's death had on him, that lost love may have been the reason he never married. In fact, when he died almost fifty years after the broken engagement, in his possession was a packet of letters from Ann.

"The fact that he kept her letters as one of his prized possessions until the end of his life kind of makes the case that he did have very strong feelings for her," notes Slaymaker. Unfortunately, Buchanan left a note attached to those letters instructing the executor of his estate to burn them without being read. No one will ever truly know the details of a relationship that may have influenced the president's life forever.

Buchanan had a love for public service, totaling ten years in the U.S. House of Representatives and twelve years in the Senate. But in the years directly before his election to the White House, he served in roles that largely kept him out of the country. Because he was serving as Franklin Pierce's minister to Great Britain, he could not become embroiled in the furor over slavery. When he ran against Republican John Fremont for president in 1856, Fremont's staunch antislavery supporters demanded withdrawal from a nation with slaveholding states. This was too radical for the country, and when Buchanan ran on a "save the Union" campaign, he won the election.

Buchanan's bachelorhood certainly did not go unnoticed during the 1856 campaign. The opposition painted a picture of a Buchanan White House as a big bachelor pad with cigarette butts on the floors, stains on the rugs, and everything else in total disarray. But Slaymaker says that wasn't the case at all. "Ironically, the Buchanan White House became a hallmark of ante-bellum elegance." His twenty-six-year-old niece, Harriet Lane, came to the White House to serve as her uncle's White House hostess.

Despite Buchanan's efforts, both sides prepared for withdrawal from one another during his four-year term. Slaymaker says, "Buchanan was elected in 1856 really with a mandate to preserve the Union through compromise and conciliation. Unfortunately, this was a time when, in all likelihood, the time for compromise had passed."

It's unfortunate that Buchanan, like the handful of presidents immediately before him, is often cast as a man with no foresight for handling the slavery issue. Slaymaker contends that Buchanan believed the U.S. Constitution and past precedence bode well for preserving the Union. "Buchanan liked to believe, as had happened in Pennsylvania, that slavery would gradually fade away on its own."

But of course it did not, and today the Buchanan presidency is but a footnote in the story of one of the country's greatest leaders. "Buchanan is often cast as a minor character in the story of Abraham Lincoln," says Slaymaker. "It almost helps to say 'When Lincoln got to the White House things were a hopeless, hopeless mess,' and they were. But Buchanan had very little control of what was going on and Congress was unsupportive of many of his ideas."

While Buchanan was rendered helpless as a lame duck president, South Carolina became the first state to secede on December 20, 1860. Buchanan urged the formation of a constitutional convention that could bring the sides together, but the idea was rejected. By February, more states had withdrawn to form the Confederacy. The Civil War began, and Buchanan soon became a convenient scapegoat for history to pin the civil problems upon.

It shouldn't be a surprise that upon Lincoln's inauguration, Buchanan said, "If you are as happy, my dear sir, on entering this house as I am in leaving it and returning home, you are the happiest man in this country." Buchanan did return to his home of Wheatland in Lancaster, Pennsylvania, where at one point the Confederate army advanced to within nine miles of his home. Local residents encouraged Buchanan to leave because they feared the southerners would burn Wheatland and take him prisoner. Slaymaker quoted the former president as saying, "If there were a thousand rebels around Wheatland I still wouldn't leave." As Slaymaker notes, "It was a sign of his determination and it also shows you how much he loved Wheatland."

Buchanan attempted to set the record straight regarding his position on the war by publishing "Mr. Buchanan's Administration on the Eve of the Rebellion," but the document received little attention. Recently, however, historians have recognized Buchanan's great devotion to averting war and his efforts to offer policies that could have brought about a peaceful settlement. Slaymaker explains, "At least the issues were clear for Lincoln once the war began. He knew that he had to prevail at any cost. Buchanan was like a man trying to hold together a house of cards that was collapsing. It was a no-win situation."

It is unfortunate that Buchanan's passion to preserve the Union is not more positively recognized. As you tour his home of Wheatland, you can't help but wonder about the passions in his life. His love for Ann Coleman left him brokenhearted, and it may have been on his mind for years as evidenced by the letters he kept.

He loved the law of the land and thought it would ultimately mend the North and South. Slaymaker says, "He had great reverence for the rule of law and for the Constitution, and I think if there were a value we could respect today, it would perhaps be that." He loved his home as well, and when there was a threat of the ex-president's being taken prisoner by the South, that love for the land led him to stay to defend it.

It would be wrong, however, to say that Buchanan's loves always left him brokenhearted. Certainly he had his share of heartaches, but it was his passion for public service that led him to serve his state and country. In the country's most difficult hour, Buchanan still had a passion to preserve the Union.

Love often drives our actions and gives our lives purpose and meaning. It can give us hope in our most trying times. It can push us forward when we have little energy to keep going. And while our loves may sometimes leave us open to the sting of defeat, Buchanan might well have agreed that, without love, he would have had nothing at all.

The Power of Words

WASHINGTON, D.C.

"Always bear in mind that your own resolution to succeed is more important than any other one thing."

—ABRAHAM LINCOLN

Did you know Abraham Lincoln . . .

...LIKED TO MAKE UNANNOUNCED APPEARANCES AT LOCAL THEATRES?

...THOUGHT THE "GETTYSBURG ADDRESS" WAS A FLOP?

...BELIEVED THE UNION HAD WON A FAMOUS SONG AS WELL AS DEFEATING THE CONFEDERACY?

"We here highly resolve that these dead shall not have died in vain; that this nation, under God, shall have a new birth of freedom, and that this government of the people, by the people, and for the people shall not perish from this earth." These are the conclusion of 272 words delivered by Abraham Lincoln at Gettysburg, Pennsylvania, on November 19, 1863. They have been spoken, memorized, and memorialized around the world, and serve as a reminder of a president who was known for his powerful words.

Edward Everett, main speaker for the event, delivered an address that covered two hours before Lincoln rose to speak that day in Gettysburg. Everett later wrote Lincoln, "I should be glad if I could flatter myself that I came as near to the central idea of the occasion in two hours as you did in two minutes." Ironically, when Lincoln had finished his address, he believed his words had failed to move anyone and that the speech was a flop.

Today people flock to sites that honor the sixteenth president in Illinois, Indiana, Kentucky, Washington, D.C., and elsewhere. In my travels I am always fascinated at people's interest in Lincoln, even outside of this country. One Lincoln guide relayed an account where a citizen of India said people still name their children after President Lincoln there.

Many of us remember his words. We are inspired by quotes like, "Always bear in mind that your own resolution to succeed is more important than any other one thing." We are amused by Lincoln's words, "No matter how much cats fight, there always seem to be plenty of kittens." His great debates with Stephan Douglas are still discussed in classrooms. We are a nation that still yearns to learn from Abraham Lincoln.

It was also Lincoln's words that played a major role in the last days of his life. Jim Lance is a historical interpreter at Ford's Theatre in Washington, D.C. and he says Lincoln loved to attend plays almost any night of the week. "Lincoln would walk the streets sometimes at night; the world was on his mind and he was trying to get away. He might come by and if he saw a playbill and it looked interesting, he would go in. If there was a back seat on the back row, whoever was sitting there might find the president sitting next to them."

There were three theatres within walking distance of the White House, and Ford's Theatre was one of them. Lincoln had been to Ford's theatre "officially" at least ten times before the fateful evening of April

14, 1865, but no one knows how many other times he might have slipped into a back row as a way to take his mind off of the Civil War.

Ironically, for a man whose words are still quoted and memorized as much as any president before or since, it was Lincoln's words in part that galvanized one man to try to kill him. The Confederate army led by Robert E. Lee surrendered on April 9. On Tuesday the 11th, Lincoln stood on the side porch of the White House before a crowd that wanted to hear the orator deliver a victory speech. Lincoln instead told the group it was not a time for a speech but instead a time for celebration, a time to talk about reuniting the nation.

As Lincoln turned to leave, he told the Marines Corp Band to play the song "Dixie," the marching song of the Confederacy. Lance reflects, "He [Lincoln] told them that the attorney general and he had decided just a day earlier that since the north had won the war, that meant they had fairly captured Dixie Land and that song belonged to the north." But Lance says there was a problem. "It's fine to do that, but the problem was, John Wilkes Booth was in the audience."

In David Herbert Donald's book *Lincoln* he writes, "Lincoln's address on April 11 triggered Booth's shift from thought to action. In the crowd outside the White House that evening, he heard the President recommend suffrage for blacks who were educated or had served in the Union armies . . . and he [Booth] vowed, 'That is the last speech he will ever make.' He urged Lewis Paine to shoot the President on the spot. When Paine refused, Booth turned in disgust to his other companion, David Herold, and exclaimed, 'By God, I'll put him through.'"

It might be quite a reach to say that those few words were enough to make a man suddenly want to assassinate the president. However, Lance, a man who has studied the subject extensively and speaks about the assassination at Ford's Theatre, contends that although

Booth hated Lincoln, it was those words that seemed to have lit the fuse for him to carry out his plot later that week. Booth had earlier plotted to kidnap the president and hold him for ransom, but with the war now over, those words may have led his mind to leap from kidnapping the president to killing him.

Three days later Lincoln made an official visit to the theatre. Lance relates, "That night they came because it was exactly five days earlier that Robert E. Lee had surrendered. It was a celebration, so he was scheduled to come that night. People in town knew about it. They sold 1,700 tickets, but they only had 1,030 seats." That same day Booth came to town to get a haircut and go by the theatre to pick up his mail (at that time actors who traveled often had their mail delivered to the theatre). He picked up those letters and learned Ford's would be hosting the president that night.

The play being performed was a British play, *Our American Cousin*. Booth knew the play and he knew that at one point in it an actor would deliver one of the funniest lines in the show, a line that would certainly garner plenty of laughter and applause. He came back that afternoon and watched the actors rehearse. He took out his pocket watch and figured the amount of time it took from the beginning of the play to that humorous delivery. He calculated the line would be delivered at about ten o'clock that evening.

The assassination of the president that night was part of a bigger planned assault on the government. George Atzerodt was to go to the hotel where the vice president was staying and kill him. He got drunk instead and never attempted the deadly mission. Lewis Powell (sometimes called Lewis Paine) was to kill the secretary of state. The secretary was recovering at his home from a carriage accident. Powell posed as a messenger from a pharmacy and entered the home. He got into the secretary's room and attempted to cut his throat. However, family and friends in the home heard the commotion and subdued the attacker before he could kill the secretary. Seward would live to later acquire the state of Alaska for the United States.

Booth delivered the fatal bullet that night at about 10:15, just as the funniest line in the show was delivered. He escaped and was not tracked down until twelve days later, on the 26th of April, about eighty miles south of the capital, when an army patrol got a tip he was hiding in a tobacco drying barn. David Harold, a conspirator with Booth, decided to surrender. They burned the barn to flush out Booth. Though the troops had been given orders to take him alive, Boston Corbett, an army sergeant, snuck up to the burning barn and began to look through the gaps in the wood sheeting. He saw Booth and fired, hitting him in the neck. The troops dragged Booth from the burning building, but he died two hours later.

Words should never be taken lightly, for they have the power to inspire as well as the power to insight violence. Lance says, "John Wilkes Booth, had he not been on the White House lawn on Tuesday the 11th, might not have heard the words Lincoln used to make him so angry. And if Lincoln hadn't made the comment about having the north win the war and therefore the song 'Dixieland' belonged to them . . . who knows? I believe that was one of the big catalysts that got Booth thinking about killing Abraham Lincoln." Had he waited another day to pick up his mail, perhaps his moment to kill the president would have passed and he would have found Lincoln to be a friend of the South.

No, Lincoln did not cause his own death or say anything wrong that 11th of April on the porch of the White House. However, it's Lincoln's words that continue to inspire people today. His words moved people to action, for better or worse. Of all the presidents, it's Lincoln above all who teaches us the power of words that inspire our actions.

George Washington, at the age of only twenty-two, surrendered to the French at this small stockade, today called Fort Necessity, on July 4, 1754. This reconstruction of the fort is part of Fort Necessity National Battlefield in southwest Pennsylvania. *Photo by Andrew McCrea.*

Thomas Jefferson used the 1,000-foot-long garden terrace at his home, Monticello, as both a source of food and an experimental laboratory. *Photo courtesy of the Monticello/Thomas Jefferson Foundation, Inc.*

James Madison and his wife Dolly resided at their home, Montpelier, in the rolling hills of Orange County, Virginia. James Madison is considered to be the "Father of the U.S. Constitution." *Photo courtesy of James Madison's Montpelier.*

The **James K. Polk** Ancestral Home in Columbia, Tennessee, was built in 1816 by Samuel Polk, James' father. The future president lived here from 1818 until 1824 when he married Sarah Childress. *Photo by Andrew McCrea.*

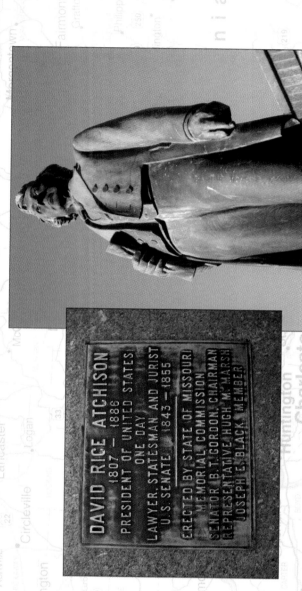

On the plaque:

DAVID RICE ATCHISON
1807 — 1886
PRESIDENT OF UNITED STATES
ONE DAY

LAWYER, STATESMAN AND JURIST
U.S. SENATE   1843 — 1855

ERECTED BY STATE OF MISSOURI
MEMORIAL COMMISSION
SENATOR B. T. GORDON, CHAIRMAN
REPRESENTATIVE HUGH M. MARSH
JOSEPH E. BLACK, MEMBER

David Rice Atchison had a long and prestigious career in politics, but he is often remembered for just one day in presidential history...March 4, 1849. His statue in front of the Clinton County, Missouri, courthouse states that he was indeed president for one day between the terms of James K. Polk and Zachary Taylor. *Photo by Andrew McCrea.*

Millard Fillmore built this small home in East Aurora, New York, in 1825. The following year he married Abigail Powers. The two met when Miss Powers, who was almost two years older than Millard, served as his school teacher. *Photo by Andrew McCrea.*

James Buchanan's Wheatland is in Lancaster, Pennsylvania. Originally built by lawyer and banker William Jenkins in 1828, Jenkins called it "The Wheatlands" because of the wheat fields that surrounded the home. Buchanan later shorted the name to "Wheatland" when he bought the property in 1848 while serving as secretary of state. This is a rear view of the home. *Photo by Andrew McCrea.*

Ulysses S. Grant, (inset) originally named "Hiram Grant," was born in this home near the banks of the Ohio River in Point Pleasant, Ohio, in April of 1822. At one time, the Grant birthplace home made a tour of the nation on a railroad flatcar before returning to its original location in the river town.

Ulysses and Julia Grant lived on the White Haven farm during the 1850s, but it remained a place to call home throughout their lives. *Photos by Andrew McCrea.*

Chester Arthur was born in Fairfield, Vermont, but the family soon moved to a parsonage a few miles outside of town. This reconstruction of the parsonage is on the site of the original home. Arthur was the northernmost-born U.S. president. *Photo courtesy of Vermont Division for Historic Preservation, President Chester Arthur State Historic Site.*

Grover Cleveland was born in Caldwell, New Jersey, the fifth of nine children born to Presbyterian minister Richard Cleveland. He was the only U.S. president to serve two non-consecutive terms. *Photo by Andrew McCrea.*

Theodore Roosevelt's Maltese Cross Cabin was his first home when he journied to Dakota Territory. Today it stands at the entrance to the South Unit of Theodore Roosevelt National Park as a symbolic representation of the cattle ranching and "strenuous life" of pioneer living that had such a profound effect upon young Theodore Roosevelt. This influence affected his conservation ethic and the course of the nation. *Photo by Andrew McCrea.*

William Howard Taft was the only man to serve as both president of the United States and chief justice of the U.S. Supreme Court during his lifetime. Today the birthplace home in Cincinnati is part of the William Howard Taft National Historic Site. *Photo by Andrew McCrea.*

Woodrow Wilson was the son of a Presbyterian minister. He was born on December 28, 1856, in the Presbyterian Manse in Staunton, Virginia. *Photo courtesy of the Woodrow Wilson Presidential Library, Staunton, Virginia.*

Calvin Coolidge was sworn into office by his father in the front room of the family home in Plymouth Notch, Vermont, in the early morning hours of August 3, 1923. Inset—In 1924, Coolidge used the dance hall above the general store, across the street from the home, as his summer White House. *Photo courtesy of the Vermont Division for Historic Preservation, President Calvin Coolidge State Historic Site.*

Herbert Hoover was born in this small home in West Branch, Iowa, on August 10, 1874. Orphaned at the age of nine, he was sent west to Oregon to live with his uncle in 1885. He graduated from Stanford University and traveled the world as a mining engineer before entering politics. *Photo courtesy of the National Park Service, Herbert Hoover National Historic Site.*

Franklin Roosevelt designed Top Cottage as a retreat from his Springwood home in Hyde Park, New York. During a famous June, 1939, picnic at Top Cottage, he served hot dogs to the king and queen of England. *Photo courtesy of the National Park Service, Roosevelt-Vanderbilt National Historic Site.*

One Vote*

GREENEVILLE, TENNESSEE

*"I intend to stand by the Constitution as it is,
insisting upon a compliance with all its guaranties . . .
it is the last hope of human freedom."*

—ANDREW JOHNSON

Did you know Andrew Johnson . . .

...WAS ALMOST LYNCHED IN HIS HOME STATE OF TENNESSEE?
...WAS A TAILOR WHO MADE HIS OWN CLOTHES?
...REMAINED PRESIDENT THANKS TO ONE SWING VOTE?

The line between courageousness and stupidity may be difficult to discern. Such was the case for two men facing tough political decisions just after the close of the Civil War. Many ridiculed their decisions, but the stand they took is still a lesson to leaders today.

The story began in Greenville, Tennessee, a small town in the eastern part of the Volunteer State, when young Andrew Johnson moved there to open a tailor shop. Ironically, the tailor trade was something he ran away from home to avoid during his teenage years. Johnson's father died when he was just a child, and his mother apprenticed him to a local tailor so that young Andrew would have a career someday. She never imagined the new career would provide him with the skills he'd need to lead him all the way to the White House.

By his mid twenties, Andrew Johnson had built a good business and a good reputation at the corner of College and Depot streets. His tailor shop was well run and well visited. He was much more than a tailor; he was actually educating himself in several different careers all at the same time. He hired people to read books to him as he worked and always made time to talk with the many political leaders who stopped by his store. Andrew Johnson was constantly around the news of the day, and he made an effort to continually keep abreast of the world of politics.

Although the tailor shop was successful, Johnson longed to run for political office and he soon set his sights on the position of city alderman. Later, he worked up the political ranks, serving as mayor of Greenville. There were bigger offices to run for, and the tailor shop was eventually left behind as he became a state representative, then governor of Tennessee, and finally a U.S. senator.

Johnson was serving in the U.S. Senate when the first southern states began seceding from the Union. Although Johnson was a Democrat from a slave-holding state, he sought to preserve the Union. In fact, when all other southern U.S. senators left Congress in favor of secession, Johnson stayed. It was a courageous decision, but a decision not without consequences. The move made him a hero in the eyes of the north, but a traitor in the eyes of many southerners. When Johnson returned home to Tennessee in 1861, he barely escaped a lynch mob as he rode the train through Virginia. Tensions were high and war was beginning to rip the Union apart. Every decision was met by fierce opposition from one side or the other. Now was the time to know what one believed in and stood for.

Johnson stood by his decision to remain in Congress. "I intend to stand by the Constitution as it is, insisting upon a compliance with all its guaranties . . . it is the last hope of human freedom," he declared.

In 1862, Lincoln appointed Johnson military governor of Tennessee. Two years later, in 1864, Lincoln selected Johnson as his vice presidential candidate. The two handily won the presidential election. Barely into his second term of office, on April 15, 1865, Lincoln was assassinated. So it was that the Democrat from Greenville, Tennessee, was sworn in as the seventeenth president of the United States.

Johnson was immediately thrust into a position in which there was no way to "win." There was bitter debate over how to reconstruct the South. Johnson opposed the views of staunch Republicans in Congress and vetoed much of their legislation. In an effort to control the actions of the president, Congress passed the Tenure of Office Act. The provision stated that a president could not dismiss a member of his cabinet without the approval of Congress. Johnson did not believe the act was constitutional and fired his secretary of war Edwin Stanton and appointed Ulysses S. Grant in his place. Johnson had not even appointed Stanton to the position; he had inherited his cabinet from Lincoln. Stanton refused to give up his position and was reinstated by the Senate in January of 1868.

One month later, Johnson again fired Stanton. Congress was furious. They brought eleven articles of impeachment against Johnson for "high crimes and misdemeanors." In order to remove the president from office, two-thirds of the Senate had to vote for his conviction. The trial began in March of 1868 and lasted two months.

The vote was a virtual deadlock. Johnson's opponents needed thirty-six votes to remove him from office. It appeared Johnson's opponents were one vote short, but one senator was still undecided . . . Senator Edmund Ross from Kansas. Ross did not announce his intentions until his name was called to state his vote. Then Ross rose and simply replied, "Not guilty."

That one vote was enough to keep Johnson in office. That one vote also spelled the end of Ross' political career. Republicans were infuriated that he would support Johnson and Ross was never elected to another office.

Today that vote is considered a courageous vote of foresight. If Johnson had been removed, it would have set a precedent that Congress could pass unpopular legislation and use it to remove a president from office. Ross saw the larger picture. His vote was costly, though. He was ostracized and attacked in his home state of Kansas. He was unable to gain reelection and died in poverty.

Johnson was certainly courageous in standing up for his view on how the reconstruction of the Union should proceed. Certainly there was fault on both sides. Johnson can be admired for not wavering during a time when strong leadership was needed. Though he sought reelection in 1868, he was not even nominated by his own party. Horatio Seymour of New York became the Democratic candidate. Ulysses S. Grant, the man Johnson had sought to make his secretary of war, defeated Seymour.

Today, most people do not even know there is a tailor shop in Greenville, Tennessee, where young Andrew Johnson learned his early lessons of leadership. However, the place marks the spot where a president would take his first steps toward the White House. This was a presidency preserved by a Kansas senator named Ross. The two would make history for their courageous votes during a difficult time. It's a lesson that still stands today.

*This story originally appeared as a part of Andrew McCrea's book *American Countryside* and has been reprinted as a part of this book on the presidents.

General Grant's Mobile Home

POINT PLEASANT, OHIO

*"I know only two tunes: one of them is 'Yankee Doodle'
and the other one isn't."*

—ULYSSES S. GRANT

Did you know Ulysses S. Grant . . .

...RECEIVED HIS BIRTH NAME BY CHOICES DRAWN FROM A HAT?
...WAS BORN IN A HOUSE THAT BECAME A "MOBILE" HOME?
...WAS SPIED UPON BY ONE OF PRESIDENT LINCOLN'S ADVISORS?

For a man as popular as President Ulysses S. Grant, it may seem odd that he lived in a mobile home. However, when you learn what kind of mobile home it was, you truly begin to understand the impact this man had on his country during his lifetime.

No matter how "big" Grant's name became, he began life in one of the smallest houses in the area. Loretta Fuhrman is curator of the Grant birthplace just outside of Cincinnati, Ohio, a sixteen-and-a-half by nineteen-foot home. She says those three hundred square feet were the family's entire living quarters. "That's the kitchen, bedroom, everything . . . and Grant's father paid rent of two dollars per month to live here."

When he was six months old, young Grant was taken to the home of his maternal grandparents, the Simpsons, who lived about twelve miles away. Fuhrman explains, "Everybody was given a slip of paper and was to write down a name they liked and they put it in a hat and the maternal grandparents got to choose the name. The name chosen was Hiram Ulysses Grant, and that was Grant's given name."

Nonetheless, Grant used that name for only a short time. When the congressman recommending him for West Point filled out the application, he thought "Ulysses" was Grant's real first name since everyone called him by some form of that name. He also supposed that Grant's middle name was "Simpson," his mother's maiden name. Grant kept the "new" name. There are conflicting stories as to why he did this. Some say he thought it appropriate to attend West Point and have the initials "U.S." Others say he did not like the fact that his real name spelled the acronym "HUG" and figured other cadets would give him a hard time if those letters were written on his trunk at the academy. Still others say he simply liked the new name better. Whatever the case, history knows him as Ulysses S. Grant, not Hiram Ulysses Grant.

Grant's military career is one that contains a great mixture of fact and fiction. Chris Eckard, chief of interpretation at the Ulysses S. Grant National Historic Site in St. Louis, Missouri, says that many visitors arrive with a perception of the president that is not entirely true. Most myths revolve around the abuse of alcohol. Eckard relates, "There is some evidence that he did drink in the 1850s when he was stationed out on the west coast at a very isolated post. But he gets a reputation in the military as someone who drank." Eckard adds that it is simply a mystery as to how much fact, if any, is in the story.

The rumors persisted well into the Civil War, perhaps perpetuated by men jealous of his success, hoping to use the gossip to keep him from ascending rank ahead of them. President Lincoln heard these stories and was concerned; before he would give Grant more responsibility in the military, he wanted to gather all the facts. Consequently, Lincoln sent Charles Dana, assistant secretary of war, to be his eyes and ears on the battlefield.

Eckard explains, "Charles Dana was sent more or less as a spy for the Lincoln administration to check up on Grant because a lot of negative things had been said about him. There were a lot of rumors persisting about him. Dana came in and gave an outside perspective of what was going on in Grant's camp and actually became an advocate of Grant's because he realized that the things being said were not true and that this was indeed a very capable guy."

Grant's success as commander of the Union troops led him to become a popular choice for president in 1868, an election he easily won. "He was somebody people could relate to," says Eckard. "One of his best qualities was that he didn't give long speeches; he gave very short speeches. In an era when politicians and orators could go on for hours, Grant's brief comments were very down-to-earth, sincere, and humble. He was a presidential candidate out of a sense of duty."

If Grant was a likeable orator, he certainly wasn't an accomplished vocalist, a fact even he admitted. One humorous account has Grant attending a concert where, after its conclusion, he was asked how he enjoyed the performance. He replied, "How could I? I know only two tunes: one of them is 'Yankee Doodle' and the other one isn't."

President Grant is sometimes cast as a man who held loose reign over his office, allowing corruption and fraud in his cabinet. Those facts can't be denied. However, many historians are now recognizing Grant's leadership skills, abilities that may have been masked by the difficult task he had of rebuilding the nation. He was very progressive in wanting to include Native Americans in the expanding nation, an idea that ran counter to many in government who simply wanted to shove them onto reservations. Grant had a desire to fulfill the ideals of the war and to handle the difficult issues of the time, but the reconstruction period greatly limited what he was able to do.

It is important to recognize Grant's great popularity in the time in which he lived. Fuhrman relates, "In 1890, the front room of the [birthplace] house, the Grant's original home, was placed upon a river barge and was transported up and down the Ohio and other rivers for people to see the president general's birthplace."

That was far from the end of journey for what would become Grant's "mobile" home. Fuhrman continues, "This little house was then taken on the flat car of a train and pulled to Columbus, Ohio, and it rested there on the fairgrounds until 1927." The home was then moved again, this time back to the spot where it had begun its tremendous journey, here in Point Pleasant, a town on the banks of the Ohio River.

That's still not the end of the story of this well traveled home. "The Ohio River flooded in the great flood of 1937 and the river rose many feet and it completely covered the building [birthplace home], all but the pitch of the roof," says Fuhrman. But as the floodwaters rose, members of the historical society quickly packed all the historic artifacts from the small house and took them to the top of a local church that stood on higher ground.

The fact that this small birthplace home has traveled so far and received so much care speaks to the great regard people had and still have for Ulysses S. Grant. As I reflect on the life of Grant, I wonder how I would fare if a spy were sent to watch my actions. Would my life be an example to others? Grant did not know that Charles Dana had been sent by President Lincoln to evaluate him, yet Dana's report eased Lincoln's misgivings. It doesn't take a spy to evaluate us; people see our actions every day whether we think they notice or not. Our actions truly do speak louder than words. What do our actions say to others?

> "I am well aware that in assuming this position I shall evoke more ridicule than enthusiasm at the outset. What may appear absurd today will assume a serious aspect tomorrow."
>
> —VICTORIA WOODHULL

Did you know Victoria Woodhull . . .

...WAS THE FIRST WOMAN TO RUN FOR PRESIDENT OF THE UNITED STATES?

...BUILT A REPUTATION ON HER TALENTS AS A FINANCIAL ANALYST AND CLAIRVOYANT?

...SPENT ELECTION DAY IN JAIL?

Geraldine Ferraro made history in 1984 when she became the first woman to be nominated for vice president by a major political party. But to find the very first woman to run for the office of president, you must go back to 1872 and a most unique woman by the name of Victoria Woodhull.

Political candidates often campaign by telling voters what they hope to do in the future for their district, state, or nation. They may use elegant words to paint a picture of a bright tomorrow. Victoria Woodhull took it a step further . . . she actually believed she *could* see the future. Yes, one of the professions of this country's first woman presidential candidate was that of clairvoyant.

Billie Luisi-Potts, executive director of the National Women's Hall of Fame in Seneca Falls, New York, recounts that Woodhull had contact with some of the "big" names of her time. Her talent as a clairvoyant and financial advisor allowed her to interact with several influential people. "She was a very charming person. She connected with Cornelius Vanderbilt and a circle of well connected financial people, which was certainly a very unusual leap for someone from her background. She must have been talented as a clairvoyant because she had an army of people who believed in her readings."

Woodhull and her sister, Tennessee Claflin, ran a brokerage house in New York City, also a rarity for the day, and became well-regarded voices in the financial district. They published a newspaper as well, *Woodhull and Claflin's Weekly*, a publication that proffered their progressive political views. Potts explains, "She was in favor of liberalization of divorce. She was in favor of equality, not just in helping women gain the right to vote but also in equality of opportunity for education and helping woman gain access to jobs in fields that were not open to them."

She met Susan B. Anthony and Elizabeth Cady Stanton, leaders in the suffrage movement, and initially gained their support. However, for Anthony, who came from a Quaker background, Woodhull's views and tactics soon strayed too far from her own forward-thinking agenda. Woodhull's support of what was called "free love" caused Anthony and others to separate themselves from full support of her campaign.

Woodhull viewed the fourteenth amendment of the U.S. Constitution as already including women with the rights of their male counterparts. In her view, women were citizens of the United States, possessing equal rights under the Constitution. Potts explains, "On the basis of her interpretation she decided to take the leap and run for office, and if you're going to run for office and you're known nationally, why not take the greatest leap possible and run for president?"

The election of 1872 was a landmark, not just for Victoria Woodhull but for the women's rights movement. In that election, Susan B. Anthony went to her hometown of Rochester, New York, to vote. Authorities soon arrested her for the illegal ballot she had cast. (It's interesting to note that most accounts state several other women voted as well, but Anthony was the only person arrested.) The ensuing trial was so controversial that the hearing was moved to another county. In response, Anthony and her supporters began what Potts describes as a "whistle stop campaign" to explain why women should have the right to vote. After all, if women could own property and pay taxes, shouldn't they have the right to vote?

It was the Equal Rights Party that nominated Woodhull for the White House. The party also made another first in presidential politics when it nominated Frederick Douglass for vice president, the first black man to be a candidate for the position. Woodhull herself spent election day in jail because of an article she had published implicating the well-respected Reverend Henry Ward Beecher as having an affair with the wife of one of his colleagues. She was arrested under the Comstock laws, which prohibited sending obscene materials through the mail, but was later acquitted of the charges.

The presidential campaign served to educate citizens and advance the suffragist cause. Susan B. Anthony never had to pay one penny of the fine for her ballot, but it took almost another half century before the nineteenth amendment finally won women the right to vote.

Ironically, the woman who first ran for president, Victoria Woodhull, quietly passed from the women's rights scene. She moved to Europe in 1877 and married a wealthy banker.

Potts says, "She knew that statistically she had no chance [to win the presidency], but she felt the idea needed to be advanced if she was going to advance this interpretation of the Constitution, that women were not excluded from the right to vote." Woodhull herself stated, "I am well aware that in assuming this position I shall evoke more ridicule than enthusiasm at the outset. What may appear absurd today will assume a serious aspect tomorrow."

This was a serious cause that deserved attention, and it was because of leaders such as Woodhull, Anthony, Stanton, and a host of others that women finally obtained the right to vote. Equally important, they advanced the cause of several related issues.

Although Woodhull's views were sometimes considered far from mainstream America, we can admire her for her dedication to a worthy cause . . . a cause that has rightfully allowed women to become an important part of every election today.

Painesville
Euclid
Cleveland
Cleveland Heights
Lorain
Elyria
Parma
Youngstown
Akron
Findlay
Ashland
Canton

No Margin for Error

FREMONT, OHIO

"My policy is trust peace, and to put aside the bayonet."

—RUTHERFORD B. HAYES

Did you know Rutherford B. Hayes . . .

…WON THE PRESIDENCY BY ONE VOTE?

…DIDN'T KNOW IF HE WOULD BECOME PRESIDENT JUST DAYS BEFORE HIS INAUGURATION?

…ADVOCATED A SIX-YEAR PRESIDENTIAL TERM"?

F or weeks after the election, the two presidential candidates waited on state and federal officials to decide how to count the votes and award electors. Challenges of fraud and corruption in the state of Florida left that state's vote in question and eventually Supreme Court justices were called upon to decide the fate of the ballots and ultimately who would become the next president. In the end, the man who claimed to win the popular vote was not the man who moved into the White House.

It's a story line from the 2000 presidential race between Al Gore and George W. Bush, but it's a script that actually played out over one hundred years ago during the presidential race of 1876. Roger Bridges is executive director of the Rutherford B. Hayes Presidential Center in Fremont, Ohio, and the tight run for the White House in 2000 put Bridges on the airwaves explaining how years ago, a president few had ever heard of, won an election that mirrored the controversial one facing the country as it entered the twenty-first century.

Bridges says, "The election itself was very close. There remains a question of who won the popular vote then just as in 2000. Many people say that Samuel Tilden clearly won the vote in 1876 and of course we know people today think Gore probably won the popular vote in the year 2000. In both cases the minority [in the popular vote] won the White House."

In fact, the final popular vote total showed Tilden winning by about 250,000 votes out of 8.3 million cast. Florida, Louisiana, and South Carolina all had votes and subsequent electors in question. In Florida, the unofficial vote result had Tilden edging Hayes by a mere 94 votes, the closest vote in any of the disputed states.

"The vote was close, but the real problem was not unlike the problems in Florida in 2000," Bridges says. "There was a lot of fraud then and now. There were people who were kept from the polls by fraud and intimidation and there were ballots where they were not sure if they had a right to vote. Other ballots had the wrong symbol on them so that people who thought they were voting for Hayes might have voted for Tilden."

Because of the high percentage of illiterate voters, pictures and symbols were often used to distinguish the candidates. For instance, a picture of Abraham Lincoln might appear over the name of the Republican candidate. Political leaders could influence the vote by swapping pictures on the ballots when they were printed. Thus, illiterate voters who thought they were voting for the Republican candidate might be voting for a Democrat if the picture of Lincoln were inserted in a different place.

By December of 1876, the U.S. House and Senate had formed a special committee of five senators, five house members, and five justices from the Supreme Court. That fifteen-member body was in charge of conducting hearings to decide the fate of the three state's electors who were in question. Thus, their decisions would decide the outcome of the presidential election. Hayes needed to win all three states in order to become president.

During February, the special committee examined the votes in each of the states in question and ultimately decided whether Tilden or Hayes had rightfully won the election in those states. The committee voted along party lines every time, tallying an 8-7 decision for Hayes in every state in dispute. The final electoral vote count gave Hayes 185 electoral votes to Tilden's 184. The senate did not confirm the electoral vote until March 2, 1877, and Hayes was sworn in during a private ceremony one day later, having won the election by a single electoral vote.

Hayes inherited a nation still deeply divided over a decade after the Civil War. Federal troops still occupied portions of the south, enforcing the policies of Reconstruction. Hayes was a believer in the use of the military to secure equal rights for all Americans and he had fought for the Union in the Civil War, even though he was forty years old and had four children at the time. He was wounded five times in battle. Yet the president ultimately believed in the need for education, not federal troops, to unite the country. He stated, "My policy is trust—peace, and to put aside the bayonet."

Bridges says, "By and large Hayes restored the power of the presidency which had been badly eroded because of Andrew Johnson and the fact that Ulysses Grant did not believe in a strong presidency. Hayes restored the power over his own cabinet; he appointed people that he believed were men of integrity." Such integrity was vital after the disputed election. Nonetheless, Rutherford B. Hayes was labeled "Rutherfraud" and "His fraudulency" by those who felt Tilden had won the election, but his impeccable character could be found in all aspects of his life, including the fact that he didn't drink or smoke, although almost all other men of the day did so.

Throughout his term in office, Hayes fervently supported the need for equal rights. He refused to accept legislative riders to appropriation bills that would have repealed laws protecting federal black voting rights. He maintained that the protection of equal rights for blacks and whites required education. Hayes said, "Let me assure my countrymen of the Southern States that it is my earnest desire . . . to put forth my best efforts in behalf of a civil policy which will forever wipe out in our political affairs the color line and the distinction between North and South."

Hayes only served one term in office, but that's the way he planned it. Bridges says, "He believed that if a president stood for re-election he would bend his views and be perceived as bending his views to secure re-election. He thought he could be both more independent and a better leader by choosing to serve only one term and that his actions would not be tarnished by others as being seen as political. At the same time, he did believe that the president should serve a single six-year term and he wished somebody would introduce that as a constitutional amendment."

Character counts, especially in a contested election won by a single vote. Hayes' integrity won him the confidence of many who at first doubted him. He believed education, not sheer force, would be the way the country would heal its wounds. No amount of education would accomplish that in a four-year presidential term, but no amount of military force would either. Character, integrity, education . . . they were all important qualities to a man who won the presidency with no margin for error.

Last of the Log Cabins

MENTOR, OHIO

"A pound of pluck is worth a ton of luck."

—JAMES GARFIELD

Did you know James Garfield

…WAS THE LAST MAN BORN IN A LOG CABIN TO BECOME PRESIDENT?

…HAD A SPRING MATTRESS THAT MAY HAVE CONTRIBUTED TO HIS DEATH?

…SELECTED ABRAHAM LINCOLN'S SON AS A MEMBER OF HIS PRESIDENTIAL CABINET?

Many a movie has used a "rags to riches" tale to capture the imagination of viewers. Although you won't find any Oscar-winning movies about this man, James Garfield made one of those big leaps in his life, a leap that sent him all the way to the White House.

"He was the last president to be born in a log cabin," says Allison Sharaba at James A. Garfield's home in Mentor, Ohio. "His parents came here from New England and built a log cabin, but his father died when he was only eighteen months old." The death of his father left his mother, brother, and two sisters to work the farm and garden to make a living.

Other presidents had been born in log cabins. In fact, political parties loved to portray their candidates as men who rose to leadership from meager roots. In the 1840 campaign, William Henry Harrison was portrayed as having been born in a log cabin when in fact he was reared in a very nice home for the day. Having a humble background and being portrayed as a man truly of the people was thought to be a winning formula for capturing an election. But Garfield did not need political spin to provide a humble background. For him, it was reality.

His mother saw potential in the young man and knew he needed an education. "The only problem was that they couldn't afford to send him [to school]. So, between his mother and his brother they were able to scrape up seventeen dollars, which sent him to school for one year," explains Sharaba. The seventeen-dollar education was equivalent to earning a high school diploma. At Geauga Seminary he eventually earned what is equivalent to a high school diploma. Garfield was about sixteen years old at the time, and he soon began an alternating semester pattern of work and school, his own system for paying his way through college. At one time, he even worked as the school janitor to make the money to earn his education. Garfield was once quoted as saying, "A pound of pluck is worth a ton of luck," a testament to his hardworking attitude.

When the Civil War began, Garfield quickly volunteered his services to the governor of Ohio, and the 42nd Ohio Volunteer Infantry was formed with Garfield at its head. Garfield earned acclaim for his leadership and bravery on several occasions, but Abraham Lincoln saw promise in other areas for the young commander. Sharaba says, "Lincoln asked him to leave the military and join Congress, saying that we have a lot of generals on the battlefield but we need some better minds in Congress." Garfield was elected to the House of Representatives in 1863, beginning a seventeen-year congressional career.

In 1880 Garfield attended the Republican National Convention to nominate his friend John Sherman, a brother of famous Civil War hero William Tecumseh Sherman. Despite Garfield's support, Sherman could not gain the majority of support needed to secure the party's nomination. After thirty-three ballots, Ulysses Grant and James Blaine drew more votes than Sherman, but neither of them could gain a majority either. On the thirty-fourth attempt, Wisconsin placed all their votes in favor of Garfield. The move began a rush for the dark horse, earning him the nomination over Grant on the thirty-sixth ballot. Thus, the man who went to the convention in support of another candidate wound up becoming the party's choice to become the next president of the United States.

During the Victorian era, presidential candidates were discouraged from actively campaigning for themselves. For the gregarious Garfield, that method of campaigning just didn't fit. "He wanted to meet people directly, rather than resting on his laurels and letting others do his talking for him. So Garfield would meet crowds of people gathered on his lawn and address them from his front porch. Over 17,000 people visited the Mentor Farm during the 1880 campaign, in contrast to the nearly 700 residents in Mentor during that time. Reporters covering these speeches dubbed the property "Lawnfield," apparently impressed by the backdrop of Garfield's campaign," says Sharaba.

The front porch campaign from his home in Mentor became very popular. "They set up a temporary train stop a few miles north of Garfield's farm lane. The people could get off the train, take the lane up to the front porch, and listen to Garfield speak, then catch the train back and be home in time for dinner! It was a very effective way to get a lot of people here."

In the election of 1880, James Garfield became the last man born in a log cabin to win the presidency. His popular vote total was a scant ten thousand more than challenger Winfield Scott Hancock, but he won handily in the Electoral College.

Unfortunately, Garfield had not even been in office four full months before he was struck down by an assassin. During that brief term he didn't have time to implement his plans for civil service reform. He barely had enough time to put together his own cabinet. Among that group was Robert Todd Lincoln, the son of Abraham Lincoln, who served as his secretary of war.

It was on July 2, 1881, that Charles Guiteau shot the president in a Washington, D.C. train station. Guiteau, an emotionally disturbed man, had stalked the president for several weeks, disappointed that he had not received a presidential appointment in Europe. Just three days short of the one-year anniversary of the shooting, Guiteau was hanged for the crime. His shot did not immediately fell the president, though, as Garfield's life hung in the balance for over two months.

During these eleven weeks, from July 2 to September 19, the country anxiously waited to learn if their president would recover from his wounds. He was taken to a summer cottage in New Jersey where, ironically, his wife had also struggled to survive a serious bout with malaria earlier that summer. Probably the saddest part of this story is that Garfield would have had a very good chance of surviving the bullet wound if not for the doctors who treated him!

Doctor after doctor came to examine the president's body and each it seemed had to probe the bullet hole again and again without ever washing their hands or sterilizing their equipment. Soon the well-meaning doctors had done damage the bullet never had, even puncturing Garfield's liver. Meanwhile, newspapers provided updates on the president's health, with a nation reading each day to learn of any recovery. Citizens offered their own remedies and debate raged as to how the president should be treated.

One of the most interesting sidelights in the debacle that occurred after the assassination was Alexander Graham Bell's attempt to use a new device to find the bullet. With the help of Simon Newcomb of Baltimore, the two began experimenting with a crude metal detector, or Transducer, with the hope of using it to find the elusive bullet. They began hiding bullets in sacks of grain and sides of beef and had success in locating the slugs.

Soon the device was ready for use on the president. However, Bell and Newcomb were disappointed when the metal detector registered a steady "hum" when its wand was passed over Garfield's body. No matter where they placed the wand, it registered "positive" while hovering over him. Discouraged, the two continued their experimentation, even returning to use the device on the president once again, only to achieve the same results.

It was only after the president's death on September 19 that it was discovered that the metal detector was in fact working correctly. It was another new invention that was causing problems . . . Garfield's spring mattress. The detector was correctly finding the metal *underneath* his body, in the new spring mattress on which he was laid.

The president's autopsy revealed that the bullet had lodged in an area that most likely would not have killed him, if it were not for the relentless probing of unwashed doctor's hands that led to infection and ultimately to death. It was a sad and possibly avoidable end to the president's life.

The message to visitors at the Garfield home in Mentor is not so much about Garfield's presidency as it is about his life. It is Garfield's rise to the White House that speaks volumes to us today. Sharaba says, "Hard work is so important. Garfield started off poverty-stricken in a log cabin and he was able to achieve the presidency because he put his mind to his work and really dedicated himself to rise above his unfortunate circumstance. I think that is something we can think of today . . . that it's important to stick to our goals and do whatever we can to accomplish them." Garfield could have used his starting point in life as an easy excuse for a lowly ending. He did not do that. Instead, he worked his way through school, using education to bring him out of poverty and eventually into the political forefront.

As one interpreter at the Garfield home told me, "It teaches us that any person in this nation can become president through hard work and dedication." Although we can only guess as to what Garfield would have accomplished in his term, we can all realize the importance of setting high goals and putting forth every bit of our effort to achieve those aspirations. For James Garfield, it was a route that led him all the way to the White House.

"Since I came here I have learned that Chester A. Arthur is one man and the President of the United States is another."

—CHESTER A. ARTHUR

Did you know Chester A. Arthur . . .

...WAS THOUGHT BY SOME TO HAVE CONSPIRED TO KILL HIS PREDECESSOR?

...HAD HIS SISTER SERVE AS FIRST LADY?

...WAS NICKNAMED "ELEGANT ARTHUR" AND HAD THE ENTIRE WHITE HOUSE REDECORATED?

T here are certainly scenic drives to be made to many presidential homes. The residences of presidents like Jefferson, Madison, and Monroe are set against the backdrop of the Shenandoah Valley. Washington's Mt. Vernon overlooks the beautiful Potomac River. The Coolidge homestead in Plymouth Notch, Vermont, is a picturesque New England village. But there's just something about the drive to a presidential birthplace that far fewer have visited . . . Indeed, one of the most beautiful drives I have ever made is the trip down a winding gravel road to the Chester A. Arthur birthplace.

I truly like to visit presidential places like this, a quaint homestead set against the backdrop of Vermont dairy farms and herds of Holsteins grazing the countryside. I arrived early in the morning when the dew was still thick on the grass and Shirley Paradee was there to meet me, opening the site up early just so I could look around at the few exhibits and interview her about the life of the twenty-first president.

The very simple building is a replica of the old parsonage where the president was born, but even that information is up for debate. "There's a controversy over where he may actually have been born, but this is definitely the site where he lived until he was two years old," says Paradee. Of all the U.S. presidents, Chester Arthur was born the farthest north, only fifteen miles from Canada in northern Vermont.

Paradee says the debate continues today with differing views over the exact spot of his birth. Arthur had relatives living just a few miles to the north in Canada. "They think Chester's mom went to visit across the border and he may have been born there. But some people think that story was just a political ploy created by his opponents," explains Paradee.

What is known is that young Chester Arthur moved with his parents several times before he was of age to attend Union College, where he passed the bar exam and went to work for the prestigious law firm of Erastus Culver. One of the most famous cases Arthur's firm handled was that of Lizzie Jennings, a black lady who was denied the right to sit in the "white" seating section of a Brooklyn street car. Although the case is rarely heard of today, it actually preceded the nearly identical Rosa Parks' case from Montgomery, Alabama, that helped spark the push for civil rights in this nation. Culver's law firm helped Jennings win her case in 1856 and won $500 in damages, a large sum of money at the time. The street car company also changed its seating policy.

In 1871 Arthur was appointed by President Grant to be collector of the Port of New York. His loyalty to the Republican Party had landed him the position in charge of more than a thousand employees in the city. There is no doubt that Arthur had ties to the powerful and corrupt New York political machine run by Roscoe Conkling. Believing in the spoils system, Arthur, as head of the customs house, was able to give countless jobs to loyal Republican supporters.

There is not evidence that Arthur was blatantly corrupt; it was probably more a case of turning a blind eye to corruption he knew was present in the customs house. Nevertheless, when President Hayes moved into the White House, he was determined to clean up some of the graft for which the previous Grant administration had been known. Part of those changes included removing Arthur from his position.

The decision made for a showdown at the 1880 Republican National Convention, with Senator Conkling's political machine pushing for Grant to be nominated as the party's candidate. Conkling's group earned the title "Stalwarts" because of their staunch republican views when compared to the reformist platform of the rest of the party. The deadlocked convention finally decided upon James Garfield as their candidate and Arthur was given the nomination for vice president, a conciliation to the Stalwarts.

Arthur's term as vice president was short lived. Only a few months into his presidency, James Garfield was shot by Charles Guiteau on July 2, 1881. Garfield initially survived the gunshot wound but eventually died on September 19. It was assassin Guiteau's words that caused some to believe that he was part of an organized plan to put Chester Arthur in the White House. After shooting

Garfield, Guiteau exclaimed, "I am a stalwart of the Stalwarts . . .
Arthur is president now." On the day Garfield passed, Guiteau wrote
to Arthur saying, "My inspiration is a godsend to you and I presume
that you appreciate it. Never think of Garfield's removal as murder. It
was an act of God, resulting from a political necessity for which he
was responsible."

Some thought these to be the words of a conspiracy, but would
Conkling's Stalwarts really go as far as to conspire to have the president assassinated? No evidence was ever presented to back up the
conspiracy charge. Most likely Guiteau, a disappointed office seeker,
acted on his own. Paradee says of the assassination, "They think
maybe somebody wanted Arthur to be president. Arthur felt very bad
about it, although people didn't think he did. I think he was determined to carry on as Garfield would have, doing the things he knew
Garfield wanted to do."

That's exactly what Arthur set out to do. In the days before
Garfield's assassination, the president and Arthur had been at odds
over civil service reform. Arthur was still in support of the views of
the Conkling political machine, while Garfield was determined to
break its power. But once Arthur took office, his views changed
and he swung his support behind the Pendleton Civil Service
Reform Act.

Publisher Alexander K. McClure said of President Chester
Arthur, "No man ever entered the Presidency so profoundly and
widely distrusted, and no one ever retired more generally respected."
The words were a tribute to a man who turned his back on the political machine that had brought him to power. They pay tribute to a
president who took a hard look at what was best for all Americans
and began to change his own views, despite some of the questionable
decisions he had made prior to becoming president.

It was a great "turnaround" for the man nicknamed "Elegant Arthur," a title he earned for his affinity for fine appearances and the latest styles. He made sure to give the interior of the White House a great turnaround during his term as well. As Paradee explains, "There's a story that he had twenty-four wagon loads of furnishings taken out of the White House so that he could redo some of the rooms the way he wanted, which was Tiffany style." Some reports say Arthur refused to move in until changes had been made, declaring the home to be a "badly kept barracks." By the time Louis Tiffany had finished the overhaul of the executive's head-quarters, the government had paid the then exorbitant fee of $30,000 for the makeover.

The president made his changes in political views and White House interiors without the benefit of his beloved wife, who passed away before he took office. Arthur's sister served as his first lady during his term. He never lost his love for his wife, though, and placed a fresh rose on the mantle every day in remembrance of her.

It's possible that Arthur's turnaround in the White House was due to the fact that he knew he was running out of time to make such a change. "He suffered from Bright's disease, an inflammation of the kidneys," says Paradee. "He didn't let anyone know he had it, outside of his physician." Treatable today, at the time Bright's disease inevitably led to death. Still, Arthur continued to serve his country without letting anyone know of his ailment. He even went to the Republican National Convention in 1884 willing to run for another term as president, even though he knew he would probably not live to see the end of that four-year period. The nomination instead went to James Blaine, who lost the election to Grover Cleveland. Just two years after leaving the White House, Chester Arthur passed away.

Arthur once said of himself, "Since I came here I have learned that Chester A. Arthur is one man and the President of the United States is another." As Alexander McClure earlier noted, "No man ever entered the Presidency so profoundly and widely distrusted, and no one ever retired more generally respected." Both statements refer to a change that took place in the life of Chester Arthur.

No matter what we may have done earlier in our lives, we always have the ability to turn our lives around. We have the choice to make changes that will cast off the old and point our lives in a positive direction. We may still bear the consequences of earlier decisions, but we have a chance to make things right from that day forward.

In a sense, that's what Chester A. Arthur did. He could easily have continued the political path on which he had trod, a journey through political graft, corruption, and as McClure said, "distrust." Maybe it was the impact of Garfield's assassination, maybe it was the magnitude of becoming the leader of the United States, but something caused Arthur to change and become the different man to which he referred. The change brought him respect and the country benefited as a result.

A Battle of Babies

"I have tried so hard to do right."

—GROVER CLEVELAND

Did you know Grover Cleveland . . .

...WAS THE ONLY PRESIDENT TO BE MARRIED INSIDE THE WHITE HOUSE?

...HAD A BABY GIRL WHO IS STILL VERY FAMOUS TODAY?

...WENT ON A HONEYMOON THAT ATTRACTED SPIES WHO HID IN THE TREES?

It was a presidential race quite literally between two babies . . . at least that's the way the newspapers depicted it. And although you may not have realized it, it was the election of 1892 between those two infants in diapers that still has its name on a small part of our world today.

The story began in Caldwell, New Jersey, a town that today has been swallowed by the network of roads that surround the New York and Newark metropolitan area. The home where Grover Cleveland was born still sits on a pleasant yard canopied by hundred-year-old trees, yet the Dunkin Donuts directly across the street gives notice that time has marched on.

Stephen Grover Cleveland was the fifth of seven children born to the Reverend Richard Cleveland, minister of the local Presbyterian Church. Grover's namesake was the Reverend Stephen Grover who once pastored the same church and who helped the young family upon its arrival to the town. With such ties to the faith, it is no surprise that Grover and his brothers and sisters read the Bible together and prayed as a family every night.

Sharon Farrell, the caretaker and historian at the Cleveland home, shares the story of a man some referred to as "Uncle Jumbo." This preacher's son was one to bend the rules and push the limits at times. Farrell relates that Cleveland's own brother once commented, "Out of all of us mother had to make more apologies to the neighbors for him. He was much more mischievous than any of us, but he was also much more industrious." "Mischievous" and "industrious" might well categorize Cleveland's early life . . . a life that contained chapters today's tabloids would feast upon.

As a teenager, Cleveland decided he wanted to be a lawyer, and he made his way to Buffalo, New York, where he studied that field. He had a tremendous memory and was able to remember much information and names. One day, as president, he would display that amazing talent by delivering his inaugural address totally from memory.

The talented lawyer found success on the banks of Lake Erie. For a time he even switched to the enforcement side of the law, serving as sheriff of Buffalo and even presiding over hangings. In 1881 he was elected mayor and the following year he became governor of the state. By 1884 he was president of the United States.

When Cleveland entered the White House at the age of forty-seven, he came to Washington having never married. Halfway into the term his marital status changed when he married Francis Folsom, becoming the only president ever to marry inside the White House.

(Tyler and Wilson both married for a second time during their terms but the ceremonies were held outside the White House.) That would seem to be a story in itself, but add to this the fact that Cleveland, aged forty-nine, was marrying Miss Folsom, aged twenty-one. He'd known his wife literally from the day she was born, as she was the daughter of his law partner.

The press learned of the couple's plan to honeymoon in Deer Park, Maryland, and set up stands in the trees near their cabin to report on the events. Newspapers contained details such as when the lights went on and off in the cabin, when they went for a walk, what they ate, and who sent them letters. The new first lady grew immensely popular with the public. Francis Folsom Clubs sprang up around the nation and huge crowds flocked to hear her speak.

While this was Cleveland's first marriage, it certainly wasn't his first relationship, and it was one of his previous encounters that loomed when he first ran for president in 1884. At the age of thirty-five, unmarried and living in Buffalo, Cleveland had taken a mistress, Maria Halpin, a lady "shared" by several other men in the community. She'd become pregnant, and after giving birth had become unstable and was placed in an institution. The baby was sent to an orphanage, and after failing to legally regain custody of her son, Halpin kidnapped the baby but was later apprehended.

At the time, Maria Halpin accused Cleveland of fathering her son out of wedlock, a charge he admitted might be accurate. The baby might not have been Cleveland's, but he was the only single man among Halpin's many "friends," and she may have thought he was the most likely to admit what had happened and to marry her. Instead, he found a family to adopt the child anonymously.

Ten years later, as governor of New York and candidate for president in 1884, the situation was brought to light. Farrell says, "What he did when faced with the scandal is refreshing to me. He told the truth." When the story broke in western New York, Cleveland sent a telegram to his supporters stating simply, "Tell the truth." Republicans seized upon the story and taunted Cleveland with the chant, "Ma, ma, where's my pa?"

Farrell reflects, "He never denied it, and that took a lot of energy out of what the public normally ends up doing, which is to prove that he's lying." Some thought the situation shameful and simply dismissed Cleveland as their choice for the White House. However, Farrell believes the majority said, "If he is up-front with us in a personal matter such as this, we can trust him to be honest with us when he's in the White House." Cleveland's desire to tell the truth at all costs must have resonated with the public, for he won that 1884 campaign.

Four years later, the issue of tariffs caused Cleveland and his new bride to lose the White House to Benjamin Harrison. Despite the fact that Cleveland won the popular vote, he failed to win the electoral majority. On Harrison's inauguration day, Mrs. Cleveland is reported to have said, "Take good care . . . of the house . . . we are coming back just four years from today." She was right. Her husband defeated Harrison in 1892.

In the election of 1892, Benjamin Harrison's grandson, Baby McGee, was pitted against the Cleveland's first child, Ruth, in political cartoons. Week after week, the two babies duked it out in the presidential baby race with baby Cleveland finally emerging victorious in the first week of November as her father, Grover, bested Harrison in real life.

Farrell explains that there were songs, plates, medallions, and a candy bar named after that winning infant. You may have thought that red and white packaged chocolate was in honor of a baseball legend, but the Baby Ruth candy bar was in fact designed to honor Baby Ruth Cleveland (some dispute this fact, although the manufacturer still maintains the candy bar was named for Ruth Cleveland). Farrell even sang one of the popular songs of the day for me:

Baby Ruth is my name
and let me say to you,
I am boss of the White House,
And of the nation too.
Politicians all say,
The first lady in the land,
Is my mama, but they're way off,
They mean little Ruth Cleveland.

After leaving the White House in 1896, the Clevelands and their five children moved to Princeton, New Jersey. There the former president had time to relax and spend time with his family, but in 1904 little Ruth Cleveland died at the tender age of twelve. Farrell says Cleveland loved his children, but he was sometimes saddened when he realized his own age would prevent him from seeing much of their lives. Cleveland wrote, "They have been such a comfort and joy to me in my old age, but I can't begin to tell you how deeply I regret I will not be here for them in later days." His last child was born when he was 66, and he died in 1908 at the age of 71.

On his deathbed, Cleveland's final words were, "I have tried so hard to do right." They were fitting words for a man citizens remembered as "Grover the Good." Farrell was right when she said we can learn much from the president who faced scandal before his 1884 election: "He had a tactic for keeping himself honest and keeping those around him honest. That was to tell the truth and not keep many secrets. It's something commendable in relationships, business dealings, and other areas of our lives . . . Simply tell the truth." It's good advice for all today.

A Family Affair

INDIANAPOLIS, INDIANA

*"No other people have a government more worthy of their respect
and love or a land so magnificent in extent, so pleasant to look
upon, and so full of generous suggestion to enterprise and labor."*

—BENJAMIN HARRISON

Did you know Benjamin Harrison . . .

...WAS THE GRANDSON OF A FORMER PRESIDENT?

...ONCE CHASED A GOAT DOWN PENNSYLVANIA AVENUE?

...WAS AFRAID OF THE ELECTRIC LIGHT SWITCHES INSTALLED IN THE
WHITE HOUSE?

Benjamin Harrison earned the nickname "Iceberg" because he could seem cold to new acquaintances, but to simply slap such a chilly tag onto his name would be to overlook a man warmly devoted to his family and country.

When you journey to the President Benjamin Harrison Home in Indianapolis, Indiana, you quickly learn of the tradition his family established in serving their country. Benjamin Harrison was only seven years old when his grandfather, William Henry Harrison, served his brief term in 1841 as our ninth president. His patriotic genealogy also included his great-grandfather, Benjamin Harrison V, a signer of the Declaration of Independence, and his father, John Scott Harrison, a congressman. Multiple generations of the Harrison family were involved in all levels of government, and Benjamin was not an exception.

Harrison became a lawyer before the Civil War drew him from his home in Indiana to join the conflict. He helped raise the 70th Indiana Regiment and rose the rank of brigadier general. When he returned home in 1865 he kept active in the Republican Party, eventually serving as a U.S. senator from 1881 to 1887. He emerged as a dark horse candidate for president in 1888 and was selected to campaign against President Grover Cleveland. In that election, less than a percentage point separated the two candidates, with Harrison on the lesser side of the popular vote. However, Harrison's electoral vote total eclipsed Cleveland handily, 233 to 168. Thus, Harrison became president without winning the popular election.

Four years later, Cleveland returned to challenge Harrison. This time, the Democratic rival not only bested him once again in the popular vote, he also won the Electoral College and returned to the White House. So, Grover Cleveland served two terms as president, but those four-year stints were separated by Harrison's trip to the Oval Office.

While Harrison was president, his wife, Caroline, obtained an appropriation from Congress that allowed for refurbishing the executive mansion. One of the improvements was the addition of electricity. The couple was apprehensive of the new convenience and the gentleman who installed the light switches was retained to turn them on and off. He remained employed at the White House for forty-two years, although he eventually graduated from "light switch duty." There are reports that the Harrisons were so concerned about an electric shock from the circuit that they left the lights on all night rather than touch the switches.

The Harrison White House was a family affair, with children and grandchildren living in the home. Grandchildren were permitted to have as many pets as they wished. One account has Harrison and three grandchildren chasing their wayward goat, Old Whiskers, down Pennsylvania Avenue. Work days were often complete at noon, allowing for more time to spend with family. There were frequent vacations, too, often to go hunting. One such trip became quite infamous when Harrison mistakenly shot a farmer's pig.

Just before the 1892 election, Harrison's wife became ill and died of tuberculosis. However, the public was not sympathetic at the polls and upon his defeat, Harrison returned to his home in Indianapolis (a home that is open to visitors today), trying to adjust to life outside the White House and without his wife. He did remarry four years later, to his wife's niece, Mary Scott Dimmick. Mary was nearly thirty years younger than he was, and the two had a baby girl. Thus, Harrison had a daughter younger than several of his grandchildren. Harrison's grown children refused to attend the ceremony uniting their father and Dimmick in marriage.

Many Americans believe they see little impact today from the Harrison presidency, yet his term may be one of the most visible of any executive. Each of the presidents can certainly be called patriotic, yet Harrison may have truly felt a heightened sense of family and national heritage. Harrison once said of his nation and its citizens, "No other people have a government more worthy of their respect and love or a land so magnificent in extent, so pleasant to look upon, and so full of generous suggestion to enterprise and labor."

Harrison had seen that respect and love demonstrated by generations before him. Not only did he have family ties to the Declaration of Independence, he had ties to the presidency itself. His family members had fought in the wars that gained and retained independence for the nation, and he certainly remembered those heroic deeds over a century later as he served his nation as president. It shouldn't be surprising, then, that many of the patriotic observances we regard as commonplace today have their roots in the Harrison presidency.

"The Pledge of Allegiance" that is recited in classrooms, at meetings, and at public events was written during his term. Harrison also signed the legislation that had the flag flown over all public buildings and schools, a tradition that remains today. As you tour his home in Indianapolis and listen to his life's story, you become aware of how important family and country were to him. No, we cannot say he was more patriotic than any other president before or since, but we can certainly understand the importance family and country played in his everyday life. He appreciated his heritage and the heritage of the United States and he had a deep love for his family, an attribute seen in several generations of Harrisons.

Although many presidents embody the values of patriotism and family, this should not trivialize their importance. Benjamin Harrison understood the value of the nation in which he lived because he remembered the men and women who helped form it. He recognized the need for family and the importance of serving one's country.

Today, each of us can work to build strong families, creating a lineage of leadership just as Benjamin Harrison experienced. We can take pride in our nation when we see our flag flying, whether it's from the county courthouse or from the surface of the moon. Most importantly, those flags remind us to continually seek ways to serve family and country, an idea President Harrison may have had in mind when he declared those stars and stripes should stand above so many buildings across our growing nation.

Nearer My God to Thee

Canton, Ohio

"That's all a man can hope for during his lifetime—to set an example—and when he is dead, to be an inspiration to history."

— William McKinley

Did you know William McKinley . . .

…Used a scarlet carnation as a special signal to his guests?
…Once studied to become a Methodist minister?
…Had a "cowboy" for a vice president?

His mother wanted him to become a Methodist minister, and William McKinley may well have thought that would be his life's work. Although the importance of McKinley's faith and the importance of God in his work would be evident throughout his life, the Civil War soon intervened and changed those pastoral plans.

McKinley's Civil War commander in the 23rd Ohio Volunteer Infantry was Rutherford B. Hayes, a man who would end up serving as president sixteen years before McKinley. A bond formed between the two men similar to that of an uncle and nephew, and when the war was over, McKinley returned to Ohio and became active in politics, serving in Congress and as governor of his state. Throughout these years, Hayes remained his mentor.

By 1896, McKinley was ready to make a run for president, utilizing a front porch campaign that brought voters to him. Rich McElroy, historian at the McKinley Museum and National Memorial in Canton, Ohio, says, "Three quarters of a million people showed up at McKinley's home during the summer of 1896. At first things didn't go too well, but soon they got it organized and McKinley was widely popular." Meanwhile, his opponent William Jennings Bryan traveled 18,000 miles in three months, an amazing journey before the turn of the century, delivering speeches across the nation.

McKinley won the contest by ninety-five electoral votes in 1896. Four years later, the same two candidates again ran against each other and McKinley held on the presidency, this time defeating Bryan by 137 electoral votes. McKinley's first vice president, Garret Hobart, died in office, and when McKinley ran for president again in 1900, Republicans chose Theodore Roosevelt, a Spanish-American War hero, to join him on the ticket.

McKinley was an expert at working behind the scenes to build solutions. As a consequence, some people believed he lacked decisiveness when in reality he may have just been working in ways unseen to the general public. Even his vice president Theodore Roosevelt once remarked that McKinley had no more backbone than a "chocolate éclair." He later apologized for the remark.

McElroy says, "His stroke of genius was working behind the scenes." He points to several instances when McKinley brought differing sides together. McKinley, in trying to heal the wounds that still existed between the north and the south after the Civil War, got the governor of Alabama and Booker T. Washington both on the same stage at Tuskegee Institute, an incredible accomplishment. At the 1896 Republican Convention, black delegates were told they could not stay in the same hotel as their white counterparts. McKinley told the hotel owner that if the black delegates could not stay, the white delegates would leave as well. All delegates were allowed to stay.

McKinley was also skilled at building consensus. Mark Lozo, education director of the Theodore Roosevelt Inaugural National Historic Site in Buffalo, New York, says, "Something I've admired about McKinley was his reputation for always being able to get along with just about anyone. It was said of McKinley that if you went to him and asked for a favor and he had to refuse you, instead of resenting him for it, by the time you left you would feel badly for having put him in such a position. He just had such a diplomatic way with people."

He also had a knack for communicating with people without saying a word. In 1876 McKinley defeated Levi Lamborn from Alliance, Ohio, in a congressional race. Lamborn, a horticulturalist, had begun growing carnations he had imported from France. He was very proud of his scarlet carnation and even gave McKinley some of them when McKinley commented how much he liked the flower adorning his lapel.

From that time on, McKinley often wore a "Lamborn Red" carnation on his lapel and even handed out extra carnations to friends and visitors. He also used the carnation as a way to "speak" without words. McElroy explains, "Many people coming in to visit the president were prompted, 'When McKinley gives you a carnation he would wish for you to bring your remarks to a close.' It really worked quite well because some people were happy just to get a flower from him." The gift of a carnation drew many conversations to a cordial close. The scarlet carnation later became the official state flower of Ohio.

Just six months into McKinley's second term, on September 6, 1901, he traveled to the Pan-American Exposition in Buffalo, New York. He greeted guests in a receiving line at the Temple of Music on the Expo grounds. Wearing his usual scarlet carnation on his lapel, he knelt to greet a young girl in line and unpinned the flower and gave it to her. Seconds later, Leon Czolgosz, a twenty-eight-year-old anarchist and unemployed mill worker, stepped forward and shot the president.

McKinley fell backward into the arms of the agents there to protect him and managed to tell them not to hurt his assailant. Today's doctors probably could have saved the president's life, for it was an infection, not the bullet itself, that killed McKinley. Eight days after he was shot, on September 14, 1901, gangrene set in around the wound and he died. Czolgosz was executed for the crime just six weeks later on October 29.

Most people were familiar with vice president Roosevelt and realized his style of leadership would vary greatly when compared to McKinley's. With the passing of the president, McKinley advisor Mark Hanna remarked, "Now that damn cowboy is president."

Before McKinley died on the fourteenth, he uttered what would be his last words, words fitting for a man who was known to hold true to the Christian values by which he had been reared. "Good-bye, good-bye, all. It's God's way," he said. "His will, not ours be done. Nearer my God to Thee, nearer to Thee."

It's important to note the Christian example by which McKinley lived. It's said that he never swore and hated to hear others use such language. He often prayed before making important decisions and attempted to live a life others might model. He once stated, "That's all a man can hope for during his lifetime—to set an example—and when he is dead, to be an inspiration to history."

In journeying to so many presidential sites, I feel it important to pause a moment to remark on not only McKinley's faith in God but the role faith played in most of our presidents' lives. Franklin Roosevelt in his Christmas Eve address in 1944 said, "Here at home, we will celebrate this Christmas Day in our traditional American way —because of its deep spiritual meaning to us; because the teachings of Christ are fundamental in our lives; and because we want our youngest generation to grow up knowing the significance of this tradition and the story of the coming of the immortal Prince of Peace and Good Will."

One of the entries in George Washington's diary reads, "Bless O Lord the whole race of mankind, and let the world be filled with the knowledge of Thee and Thy Son, Jesus Christ." Likewise, it was John Adams who said, "It must be felt that there is no national security but in the nation's humble and acknowledged dependence upon God and His overruling providence."

Lyndon Johnson also spoke of the importance of prayer when he said, "The men who have guided the destiny of the United States have found the strength for their tasks by going to their knees [in prayer]." And it was President Warren Harding who commented on the importance of God when he said, "It is my conviction that the fundamental trouble with the people of the United States is that they have gotten too far away from Almighty God."

Every president is human, and even those who spoke of their faith certainly made errors in judgment at times. Yet it is important to note the role faith played in shaping many of their decisions. In many cases, it was this underlying strength that helped them overcome the tremendous weight of their office. Faith remains as the great foundation that provides strength for living and hope for the future, even after death, and it was exemplified in McKinley.

McKinley's "behind the scenes" leadership is an example to many as well, including McElroy. "I feel he was certainly Ohio's greatest president," he says. "McKinley's style was quiet effective leadership . . . we'll get it done, I don't care how it gets done, and I don't care who gets the credit. This is the way it's going to be."

Quietly leading and solidly resting upon faith, McKinley's life and leadership are still an example today.

Four Hundred Days

MEDORA, NORTH DAKOTA

"I never would have been president if it had not been for my experiences in North Dakota."

—THEODORE ROOSEVELT

Did you know Theodore Roosevelt . . .

...LOST BOTH HIS WIFE AND MOTHER ON VALENTINE'S DAY OF 1884?

...WAS SHOT IN THE CHEST BY AN ASSASSIN BUT FINISHED HIS SPEECH BEFORE GOING TO THE HOSPITAL?

...OWNED A CATTLE RANCH IN THE NORTH DAKOTA BADLANDS?

He would become one of our nation's most highly regarded presidents, a man whose face is even a part of Mt. Rushmore today. But few people know of the four hundred days Theodore Roosevelt spent in the Dakota badlands, four hundred days that would give him time to reflect on what he wanted to make of his life.

Theodore Roosevelt was born to a well-to-do family in New York City in 1858. Due to his sickly nature as a child, most of his education took place in the home before he attended Harvard. He had every reason to simply rest upon the wealth and good name his family had built.

In 1880 he married Alice Hathaway Lee and the next year was elected to the state legislature in New York. But "T.R.," as many called him, was a man who yearned for more than everyday life in the Empire State. Bruce Kaye, chief naturalist at Theodore Roosevelt National Park in North Dakota, says, "He'd heard about the bison that were disappearing out here so he wanted to come out to, as he said, 'bag one of those critters' before they were hard to get."

T.R. arrived in what is today the west central North Dakota bad-lands in the fall of 1883, and before his twenty-one-day buffalo hunting trip had ended, had become so enchanted with the area that he invested in a cattle ranch with Sylvane Ferris and William Merrifield. His duties as a state assemblyman required him to return home, so Ferris and Merrifield managed his cattle operation in his absence.

By the time he returned to the ranch in 1884, much had changed in his life. Kaye says, "When he came out here in 1884, it was with a heavy heart. His wife and his mother had died on the same day, Valentine's Day. A political defeat also gave him some thought that maybe he needed to think about other things to do."

Over the course of the next three years he would spend occasional time on his ranch in the Dakota badlands, and in 1886 he remarried. By 1898 he had sold his ranching interests. "Altogether during this four-year period he was out here intermittently, some say at most four hundred days. That's even stretching it because many of those days he was off in other territories hunting and meeting people," explains Kaye.

Yet it was those four hundred days that influenced his future. Kaye continues, "T.R. was somewhat of a snob when he came out here. He didn't know how to deal with people very well. But out here he realized that he had to listen to his help, he had to take part in what he called the 'strenuous life,' and through learning how to deal with people through hard work, it helped him gain the presidency." In fact, Roosevelt would later state, "I never would have been president if it had not been for my experiences in North Dakota."

The experience fueled Roosevelt's love for the outdoors and his love for life. Mark Lozo, education director at the Theodore Roosevelt Inaugural National Historic Site in Buffalo, New York, notes, "He believed in living life to its fullest and never backing away from any challenge and always working your hardest toward anything you do. He embodied that throughout his entire life. In his sixty years he probably did enough to fill about four or five ordinary lives."

Roosevelt was truly a man who could fill four or five lives with his many adventures. Imagine Roosevelt wearing his spurs, belt buckle, and pearl-handled revolver made by Tiffany's that cost over a thousand dollars in today's money. Think of the future president leading a charge up Kettle Hill during the Spanish-American War. Dream what it was like for T.R. to lead a nine-hundred-mile exploration of the "river of doubt" in the Amazon of Brazil (a trek in which his party became ill and he almost died, although the government later renamed the river Rio Teodoro in his honor).

Roosevelt's efforts to preserve the environment also grew from his experiences ranching in the badlands. In a speech delivered in Dickinson, North Dakota, in 1886 he said, "It's not what we have that will make us a great nation; it's the way in which we use it." It was Roosevelt who helped create many of the country's great national parks. 218 acres of his badlands ranch are part of Theodore Roosevelt National Park today.

Roosevelt's ranching experiences shaped the tough and determined nature he would need for his many adventures, not to mention the presidency. These qualities showed up in some of the most unexpected places. In 1912, while running for election on the Progressive or "Bull

Moose" Party's ticket, Roosevelt was shot by saloonkeeper John Schrank as he delivered a speech in Milwaukee. The bullet hit him in the chest but was slowed by a thick manuscript in his shirt pocket. Roosevelt completed the delivery of his ninety-minute speech before a capacity crowd before going to the hospital. He remarked, it "takes more than a bullet to stop a Bull Moose."

I have spent little time speaking of Roosevelt's years as president. It's not because they were unimportant. After all, he is considered by historians to be one of our greatest leaders. However, few people know the story of Roosevelt's ranch and the four hundred days in North Dakota that shaped the rest of his life.

"People say it wasn't the amount of time out here, but its intensity. He immersed himself in the land, the people, the work, and he learned a lot of lessons that he took to the White House," says Kaye. After the death of his wife and mother, he retreated here to mourn but also to refocus on what he wanted to do with his life. As Roosevelt said, it was his time on the ranch that made the presidency possible.

We too should pause to reflect and refocus, taking time to see how we can use our lives to positively affect those around us. It's a lesson learned by Roosevelt on his four hundred days on the ranch.

Plump and Full of Joy

CINCINNATI, OHIO

"I can hardly remember ever being president."

WILLIAM HOWARD TAFT

Did you know William Howard Taft . . .

...LED TWO OF OUR THREE BRANCHES OF GOVERNMENT?

...HAD A COW THAT GRAZED THE LAWN AT THE WHITE HOUSE?

...ESTABLISHED THE PRECEDENT OF THROWING OUT THE FIRST PITCH AT A BASEBALL GAME?

I t's the most asked question at the William Howard Taft home in Cincinnati, Ohio, a query that fascinates young and old alike, seeking an answer that will finally satisfy their curiosity. Forget the fact that Taft was the only man to serve as president and later as chief justice of the Supreme Court. People simply want to know, "Was Taft our largest president?"

Kerry Wood has probably answered that question well over a thousand times, and while he will give you an answer to your question, he'll quickly tell you much more about a remarkable man who did something no other person may ever do…lead two of our nation's three branches of government.

Taft was always an over-achiever. Wood, an education specialist at the Taft National Historic Site, explains, "His mother used to be a teacher, so she was kind of the disciplinarian of the family, making sure they didn't settle for a 'B' in class. Even as Taft went on to Yale he would graduate with the second highest score in his class, which wasn't easy to do."

Such high marks helped Taft rise through the law and judiciary ranks quickly, becoming a federal circuit judge at the age of thirty-four. Although his love always seemed to be the law rather than politics, people clamored to get Taft to serve in political positions, using his sharp mind in government. In 1900 President McKinley sent him to the Philippines as the chief civil administrator. He proved a very capable administrator, helping restart the nation after war by building roads, schools, and aiding the economy.

It was while in the Philippines that Taft was given a tempting offer, especially in light of his love for the judiciary. Wood says, "While he was in the Philippines he was offered a seat on the United States Supreme Court on several occasions, but he declined. Even though he had his personal goals, he didn't let that stop him from doing the public good, and that's what William Howard Taft was really all about."

When Theodore Roosevelt became president in 1901 upon the death of William McKinley, he sought to bring Taft into his cabinet. In 1904, Taft became secretary of war and "heir" to the Oval Office, or at least that's what Roosevelt hoped. In 1908, those wishes came true when Taft defeated William Jennings Bryan for president. However, those presidential wishes were probably more strongly held by Roosevelt and Taft's wife and family than by him. The judicial branch was his love, and his skills were probably a better fit for a position in that branch.

Taft's inauguration in 1909 began four long years in which he ultimately had to campaign against the man who once so badly wanted him to become president. By the midway point of his term, the views of Taft and Roosevelt had grown apart. Perhaps it was Taft running the country his way; perhaps it was a change in views on the part of both men. It was probably a combination of the two. By the time the election of 1912 was held, Roosevelt was running on the Bull Moose ticket, campaigning against Taft. This split in the Republican Party helped Woodrow Wilson become president. Taft finished third in the three-way race, carrying only Utah and Vermont. Taft remarked, "I'm glad to be leaving the office because it's the loneliest place to be."

Despite his defeat, Taft finally achieved a dream he may have had from his early years when in 1921 President Harding appointed him chief justice of the Supreme Court, a position he held until 1930. To this day, he remains the only person ever to lead two of the nation's three branches of government, serving as president and later as chief justice of the Supreme Court. Taft remarked, "I can hardly remember ever being president."

So . . . I've made you wait for the weight of Taft. Was President Taft our largest chief executive? At 330 pounds he most certainly was. It seems he was always on the chubby side. His mother once wrote, "He is a plump baby and full of joy." There is a story that as president he got stuck in his bathtub, but the tale is in question. We do know that the bathtub he later had installed in the White House was large enough for four men to pose inside for a photograph.

It wasn't that Taft was sedentary, either. He walked four miles each day while he was chief justice. He enjoyed getting outside and being active, and one of his more enjoyable presidential tasks was establishing the tradition of throwing out the first pitch to begin a baseball season.

He also had the honor of being the last president to graze a cow on the lawn of the White House. "The cow's name was Pauline Wayne, and if you can imagine back in the early 1900s driving down Pennsylvania Avenue and seeing a pet cow out on the presidential lawn. What a sight that would be today," laughs Wood. It was the last "large" animal to reside on the executive pasture.

Taft certainly had a love for life and a yearning to give back to the nation he served, a quality he had known since childhood. "I want people to leave here knowing the strong upbringing Taft had from his family. They really cared about the integrity of this family and giving back to their community and that's something we need to do in our current days and times," says Wood.

The fact that Taft never lost sight of his goal of serving on the Supreme Court also speaks to his determined attitude. More remarkable is the fact that he passed up the opportunity earlier in life because he felt an obligation to serve the U.S. government in the Philippines. His personal goals did not come at the expense of those he served. In the end, he not only reached his goal, he served his nation in a way no man or woman may ever do again, by leading two of our three branches of government.

Seeing Farther
Staunton, Virginia

"The world must be made safe for democracy."

—Woodrow Wilson to Congress,
seeking a declaration of war

Did you know Woodrow Wilson . . .

...Saw his church used as a military hospital during the Civil War?
...Was president of Princeton University?
...Predicted how World War I would lead to World War II?

He was born into a most loving home, but he grew up in a most hated time. Woodrow Wilson, the son of a Presbyterian minister, was born on December 28, 1856, in Staunton, Virginia, but his family moved to Augusta, Georgia, soon after. Patrick Clarke, executive director for the Woodrow Wilson Presidential Library Foundation, says some of Wilson's first memories were of a nation breaking apart. "When he was in Augusta, Georgia, there is a documented account of family history where he was standing out in the front yard playing and he heard two men say

Abraham Lincoln had been elected and that means war, and he came in and asked his father what that meant." His parents cared for those wounded in the war that ensued, using the church as a hospital. They were images Woodrow Wilson would never forget.

Wilson attended Princeton University and graduated in 1879. He continued his pursuit of education and just over two decades later returned to his alma mater to become president of the university in 1902. He brought many new teaching methods to the university, and by 1910, the popular university president was asked to run for governor of New Jersey. Not only did he win the election, but two years later he was the Democrat's choice to run for president of the United States. In that 1912 election, he garnered under forty-two percent of the vote but won in forty of the forty-eight states, besting both William Howard Taft and Theodore Roosevelt.

Although President Wilson is often associated with World War I, his accomplishments domestically shouldn't be overlooked, among which were the establishment of the Federal Reserve and strengthened child labor laws. Sadly, his wife Ellen died on April 6, 1914, just over a year into his first term. Wilson remarried in December of the next year, wedding Edith Galt, a widow whose husband had died in 1908. Clarke notes, "He was always very close to the women in his life. His three daughters had a major influence on his life." It was Wilson who signed the law giving women the right to vote. Clarke says it was partly because his daughters "really laid into him."

But war was the chief concern during Wilson's time in office, and he vowed to keep the U.S. from entering the conflict. It was a time when he reflected back to his childhood memories. Clarke says, "When he is trying his best to keep the United States from entering the Great War, and a lot of the members of Congress are hammering the tables calling for a declaration of war from the president and wondering why he won't do that, the president was known to say, 'I've seen war; I've seen what war can do; it's not something we should take lightly.'"

In 1916 Woodrow Wilson was re-elected on the slogan, "He kept us out of war," but the situation soon grew worse. The most notable event was a German telegram intended for the president of Mexico that was intercepted and deciphered by the British. In part it read, "We [Germany] intend to begin on the first of February unrestricted submarine warfare. We shall endeavor in spite of this to keep the United States of America neutral. In the event of this not succeeding, we make Mexico a proposal or alliance on the following basis: make war together, make peace together, generous financial support, and an understanding on our part that Mexico is to reconquer the lost territory in Texas, New Mexico, and Arizona."

With American sentiments now turning in support of entering the war, President Wilson also changed his stance, stating, "The world must be made safe for democracy." The Senate adopted a declaration of war on April 4, 1917, with the House following two days later. In January of 1918, Wilson delivered to Congress his Fourteen Points, the goals to be accomplished as a result of the Great War. One of those points was the formation of a world body called the League of Nations to help resolve matters and avert war.

Little of Wilson's plan was adopted in the peace treaty that was signed at war's end, though. Wilson returned from Europe and traveled the nation to garner support for the League of Nations but he suffered a major stroke while in Colorado. Clarke says the condition tended to intensify the president's personality. "Wilson's stubbornness and his resolve really are magnified at that point and he refuses to compromise anything about the League of Nations." Congress ultimately rejected the Unites States' participation in the body.

Despite the failure, Wilson was visionary as he foresaw how current events would shape world politics in a couple of decades. "At the peace treaty in France he predicts that if Germany is not treated correctly and brought in along with this process, that down the road another generation, there will be another major war that will engulf the entire world, and that comes true," says Clarke. Although Wilson's proposed League of Nations failed, the United Nations was formed after the second world conflict.

It was Wilson's visionary leadership that often leads him to be ranked as one of the most effective presidents. His foreign policies not only shaped the country and world after World War I, they influenced presidents throughout the twentieth century. Clarke notes, "I think one of the things Wilson is noted for is that vision for world peace. I think that's probably the most important legacy that Wilson had was his vision."

Wilson's vision was not something "dreamed up" by historians years later; it was evident to the people of his time. In 2001 I sat with my grandfather, Maurice McCrea, a man whose stories and wisdom I had listened to almost every day growing up on the farm. I decided to ask him about the presidents elected during his lifetime (he'd seen several, as he was born during the Theodore Roosevelt administration in 1903), and ultimately I asked the question, "Who was the greatest president that you remember?" I expected my granddad to answer "Truman," since he always seemed partial to the man who had also grown up on a Show-Me state farm. Surprisingly, he answered, "I believe that would be Woodrow Wilson." I asked why and he simply replied, "He could see farther."

While we can't predict the future, we can certainly live life in view of the future, and for that quality, President Woodrow Wilson will long be remembered.

Mother's Day

MARION, OHIO

*"I have no trouble with my enemies . . . but my friends . . .
they're the ones that keep me walking the floor nights."*

—WARREN HARDING

Did you know Warren Harding . . .

...GAMBLED AWAY THE WHITE HOUSE CHINA?
...BOUGHT HIS HOMETOWN NEWSPAPER WHEN HE WAS ONLY NINETEEN?
...HONORED HIS MOTHER EVERY SUNDAY OF HIS LIFETIME?

Some presidents dread the media, but even if Warren Harding didn't always like them, at least he understood them. He was only nineteen years old when he bought his hometown newspaper, the Marion Daily Pebble. It was a business he would own until the day that publication could print he had become president of the United States.

Today Melinda Gilpin, the manager of the President Warren Harding home historic site, says, "Even as president, he said that every day at 3:30 he was thinking about the guys putting the newspaper to bed in Marion." He avoided running critical stories if possible and was known for his amiable attitude. It is said that he never fired a single person in all the years he owned the paper.

Both of his parents were an inspiration to him and both practiced medicine. Gilpin relates, "He was the first president born after the Civil War. His father was a drummer boy for the Union army." Warren was the oldest of George and Phoebe Harding's eight children. The fact that Warren's mother practiced medicine was very rare in those days, and it may have been just one of the reasons he always seemed to pay his mother special love and reverence.

From the time he was about six years old, he brought his mother a bouquet of flowers every Sunday. This became a tradition he never allowed to lapse. If he was out of town as a state senator or lieutenant governor, he hired someone to bring her those flowers. Gilpin adds, "They say even in the White House, years after her death, he had a bouquet of flowers on his desk every Sunday in remembrance of his mother."

Although presidents often respect their mothers, Gilpin says the honor Harding paid his mother really spoke of the difference she seemed to have made in his life. "Harding was very close with his mother. She was seen as a very loving, caring person and by all accounts was what really held the family together, the strength of the family."

Over 600,000 people came to Harding's Marion, Ohio, home during 1920 to hear him speak from his front porch. Harding was the third and last president to wage a front porch campaign (Garfield and McKinley were the others). The town was too small to hold the crowds, so the usual agenda was to have those citizens stay in a number of surrounding cities the night before and then ride the train into Marion the next morning. Gilpin says, "You would march down here in a parade-style atmosphere with bands playing and flags waving and hear Harding give his campaign speech." Onlookers were assigned an eating place in town before boarding trains to leave for their homes.

Harding's looks and friendly hometown nature played well before those that traveled to hear him speak, and he won a landslide election. Unfortunately, scandal is often the first thing associated with his term. Harding's secretary of the interior, Albert Fall, went to prison for taking bribes for naval lands to be drilled by oil companies in a case that became known as the Teapot Dome scandal. Harding's veterans bureau chief embezzled money and was sent to prison as well.

Harding's fault was that he was too trusting of some of those he appointed to key cabinet positions. In fact, several of them were or became his poker-playing buddies. The group would gather in the White House and smoke, chew, and gamble for hours at a time. In one poker game, the president even gambled away a set of china used in the residence of the White House!

There were also honest, hard-working men in the Harding White House, people like future president Herbert Hoover, who was known for his excellent leadership in the Department of Commerce. Harding himself made policy decisions that were admirable. One of his earliest accomplishments was the institution of a budgetary system for the Federal Government, which did not exist. He also founded the Veterans Bureau, which was to guarantee medical treatment to injured veterans of World War I. During his presidency, tax rates were reduced by nearly twenty-five percent for average Americans, and nearly a quarter of the federal debt was paid. In 1922 he traveled to Birmingham, Alabama, and gave a speech calling for an end to racial segregation, a speech far ahead of its time.

In June of 1923, the president and first lady made a trip to Alaska and the west coast. While on that trip, Harding, who suffered from high blood pressure, an enlarged heart, and congestive heart failure, began to feel ill. While in San Francisco he died of either a stroke or heart attack in his hotel room. He probably knew only pieces of the scandals his cabinet had initiated during his two and a half years in the White House.

300,000 people came to Marion to pay their respects to Harding. Gilpin says, "It's important to remember that he was a very popular president in office. We see him as someone who was unpopular and in some cases considered the worst American president, but the people who lived in that time really approved of the way he was doing his job." She also points out that Harding's death never allowed him to answer the charges history levels against him today.

Harding once said, "I love to meet people. It is the most pleasant thing I do; it is really the only fun I have. It does not tax me, and it seems to be a very great pleasure to them." Ironically, it was Harding's friends that blemished his shortened term. He commented, "I have no trouble with my enemies . . . but my friends . . . they're the ones that keep me walking the floor nights."

Many of our presidents owe much to their parents, but Harding's relationship with his mother is striking. Not only did he recognize the significant role she had played in his life, he thanked her for it during her lifetime and remembered it throughout his own. That may have been where President Harding learned the skill of meeting people and building friendships. We too should always be mindful of the role our parents and families play in molding our lives and realize the ability we have to positively shape the lives of those who follow.

"I have never been hurt by anything I didn't say."

—CALVIN COOLIDGE

Did you know Calvin Coolidge . . .

...WAS SWORN INTO OFFICE IN THE MIDDLE OF THE NIGHT?

...DID FARM CHORES IN A THREE-PIECE SUIT?

...WON A BET WITH A LADY AT A DINNER PARTY THANKS TO HIS SILENCE?

I t was a bright, warm afternoon when William Jenney and I sat down just across from the general store in Plymouth Notch, Vermont. This peaceful little town had just twenty-nine residents back in the early 1900s. Today those residents are gone, but thousands still flock here to see the home where the little town's most famous family lived.

"He was born here on the Fourth of July in 1872. He was, incidentally, the only president to be born on Independence Day," says Jenney, administrator of the President Calvin Coolidge State Historic Site, as we opened our conversation about the man who was sworn in as the thirtieth president of the United States just a block down the street in the family residence.

Calvin Coolidge was born to a farm family in rural Vermont, although his father did serve in several different positions outside of agriculture such as the local justice of the peace and as notary public. Calvin's father was also the general storekeeper, deputy sheriff, a state senator, and served on Vermont Governor William Stickney's staff. Calvin grew up on the family farm and went to Amherst College in Massachusetts to be educated and study law. After graduation, he read the law at a Northampton, Massachusetts law firm. He ran for public office and slowly worked his way up the political ladder, eventually becoming president of the state senate, lieutenant governor, and governor of Massachusetts.

It was an event in Boston in 1919 that would prove his worth as governor and as a national political candidate. During that year, he helped settle a police strike in the city that brought his name to attention far outside the state. The very next year, at the Republican National Convention in 1920, there was strong support for the politician from Plymouth Notch to be selected as the party's presidential candidate. Warren Harding ended up winning the nomination, but the solid undercurrent of support for Coolidge won him a spot as the vice presidential candidate on the ticket.

In 1923 as President Harding made a tour of Alaska and the West Coast, he became ill and died of a stroke in San Francisco. Coolidge was in Plymouth Notch with his family on August 2 when Harding passed away, but there was a period of several hours before Coolidge was sworn in as the nation's thirtieth president. Jenney recounts, "There was only one telephone in the village and that was in the general store. Government officials tried to call the store with the news that President Harding had died, but the storekeeper had gone to bed and didn't hear the phone ringing. They finally had to call

Bridgewater Corners, the next town up the line, from where someone drove the six miles back to Plymouth Notch and delivered the message at the Coolidge Homestead.

It was the middle of the night at this point and the new president needed to be sworn in immediately, so a call was made to Washington to see what to do. "The attorney general said it was permissible for Colonel John, the president's father, to administer the presidential oath of office in his capacity of notary public. This all happened at 2:47 in the morning, August 3, 1923, by the light of a kerosene lamp." Coolidge simply went back to bed after being sworn into office, so he could get up early that morning to return to Washington, D.C.

It was a fitting way for the man with rural roots to become president, with Calvin's father swearing in his son in this town of twenty-nine people. The town awoke that morning to a new president, and ultimately to a flood of tourists when Coolidge selected Plymouth Notch as his summer White House in 1924. In those days, the location of the summer White House was frequently changed every year. Indeed, Coolidge had five different summer locations during the course of his administration.

As Jenney looked over a collection of early photographs, he reflected on what life in Plymouth Notch was like that summer in 1924. "You can imagine what an impact it was when one day a newspaper reporter counted between four and five thousand cars parked out here in this neighboring field. That was just Vermonters' Day, when Vermonters came to see their native son as president." All those cars probably pushed the crowd that day to well over ten thousand, quite a difference for a village that normally numbered in mere double digits.

Coolidge picked up the nickname "Silent Cal" because of his quiet nature. In many ways it was his image that spoke louder than words. Jenney says, "He enjoyed wearing his grandfather's frock when he helped out on the family farm. This frock was a very practical garment to keep your clothes from getting dirty. However, when Coolidge became president, some of the press thought this was a made-up costume to accentuate his humble beginnings. So Coolidge decided to wear a three-piece suit doing everything. As president you often see him haying and fishing in a three-piece suit." Thus Coolidge probably became the most formal looking farmer and fisherman in history.

Certainly Coolidge was not into idle chitchat, but if you got him on the right subject he could bend your ear on topics such as education or fishing. A famous story from when he was vice president goes that a woman seated next to him at a dinner party told him she had a bet she could get more than two words out of him. His reply to her was, "You lose." But to put it in perspective, Coolidge gave more presidential news conferences than any other president up to that time. He also wrote all his own speeches.

Coolidge once commented, "Four-fifths of all our troubles in this life would disappear if we would only sit down and keep still." However, Coolidge did not mean that leaders should sit still and do nothing in times of crisis. "No person was ever honored for what he received," Coolidge also said. "Honor has been the reward for what he gave."

Some have criticized Coolidge's approach to the presidency as setting up the country for the market crash and depression that began in 1929. Looking back, his support of tax relief for the wealthy and his lack of support for legislation that would have helped farmers certainly did not help the situation. However, recent scholars cite the fact that Coolidge reduced the national debt by a third, and that during his administration most Americans paid no federal taxes. The "Roaring Twenties" are generally considered one of the most prosperous eras in U.S. history and Coolidge led the nation during five and a half years of that time.

Part of Coolidge's quietness may have come from the sadness he felt when his sixteen-year-old son, Calvin Jr., died during the 1924 presidential campaign. It was an unusual set of circumstances that all began when the boy got an infected toe from a blister he developed while playing tennis. Because of Coolidge's nature, the public may not have known just how much the event impacted his life and the rest of his time in the White House. Coolidge later wrote, "With the death of Calvin Jr. the power and glory of the presidency left with him."

That event, most likely, led Coolidge not to run for re-election in 1928. In typical fashion, he delivered the news in the fewest words possible. At that time, the press submitted questions ahead of time in writing. Coolidge was in South Dakota in the summer of 1927 and he simply issued the press a scrap of paper that said "I do not choose to run for president in 1928." That was it. Nothing more was said.

We can learn much from Coolidge and his quiet, straightforward leadership. As Yogi Berra said, "You can observe a lot just by watching." Coolidge usually listened and thought before he spoke. He meant it when he said, "I have never been hurt by anything I didn't say." It was the type of motto he lived by.

The lessons he learned growing up on the family homestead in rural Vermont were lessons he never abandoned. When the press thought he was trying to put on a show by doing his farm chores in humble clothes, he simply made a joke of their views by dressing up to do what he normally did. In fact, Coolidge wrote in his autobiography, "In public life it is sometimes necessary in order to appear really natural to be actually artificial."

Certainly each of us should voice our opinions, take a stand, and try to make a positive impact in the world. But many times we can learn from the example of the Coolidge presidency: sometimes fewer words and quieter actions may actually make a larger and more lasting impact on society.

The Great Humanitarian
West Branch, Iowa

"A voluntary deed is infinitely more precious to our national ideas and spirit than a thousandfold poured from the Treasury."

—Herbert Hoover

Did you know Herbert Hoover . . .

...Was orphaned at the age of nine?
...Traveled around the world as a mining engineer?
...Donated his entire presidential salary to charity?

There is certainly a great deal of irony in Herbert Hoover's life. In the United States he is often portrayed as a man who did not do enough to help those in need during the Great Depression. Yet, in many other nations around the world, he was and still is regarded as a man who was devoted to helping the less fortunate. Resolving the differences between the stories helps one gain a better understanding of the man born in West Branch, Iowa, on August 10, 1874.

By the time Herbert Hoover was ten years old both his father and mother had passed away, his father from a heart attack and his mother from pneumonia. After spending a year with relatives in West

Branch, Herbert was sent to live with his uncle in Newberg, Oregon, in 1885. The Hoovers were Quakers, and Herbert always remembered the values he learned early in life. He said, "In consequence of plain living and hard work, poverty has never been their [the Quakers] lot."

Hoover attended Stanford University and majored in geology, graduating in 1895. His work as a mining engineer was a career that literally took him around the world. In 1897 he worked in Australia, but in 1899 he was offered a better paying position in China. The trip from Australia to China included a detour back to the U.S. where he married Lou Henry, a geology student he had met while a student at Stanford. The couple was wed, and the same day of the marriage they traveled to meet the steamer that took them to China. Over the next fifteen years, the Hoovers traveled to countries around the globe, with Herbert eventually owning his own engineering firm, a business that helped him earn great wealth and a good reputation even outside the engineering world.

When war broke out in Europe in 1914, Hoover was in London and his role began to change from that of mining engineer to humanitarian. He helped organize the evacuation of 120,000 Americans trapped in Europe by the war. He also helped organize the Committee for the Relief of Belgium, which brought food, medicine, and other supplies to citizens of that country. In 1917, when America entered the war, President Woodrow Wilson appointed Hoover as U.S. Food Administrator. He coordinated efforts to conserve food at home while providing food and supplies to American troops and their allies. The term "hooverize" was coined when Hoover asked citizens to adopt meatless Mondays and wheatless Wednesdays. His efforts helped cut food consumption by fifteen percent without rationing.

At the end of World War I, Hoover was appointed head of the American Relief Administration, an organization responsible for helping meet the needs of those devastated by the war. In 1921 aid was extended to Russia, and when Hoover heard of objections that he was helping to support Bolshevism, he said, "Twenty million people are starving. Whatever their politics, they shall be fed!" His leadership in directing such programs made him the choice of presidents Harding and Coolidge to be secretary of commerce.

In 1928, Hoover ran as the Republican candidate for president and easily defeated Democrat Alfred Smith, but not even a year into his term, the stock market plummeted during the last week of October, 1929. In just two months the market lost forty percent of its value, and by the time it hit bottom in July of 1932, it had lost eighty-nine percent of its worth. Unemployment rates climbed, and in 1932 over twelve million people, or about twenty-five percent of America's workforce, were unemployed.

Carol Kohan, past superintendent of Herbert Hoover National Historic Site in West Branch, says of Hoover, "He was the most popular man in the country coming in and going out quite the opposite." To many Americans, President Hoover appeared to be reluctant to have the federal government come to their aid. Kohan says Hoover's views on how to deal with the depression had their roots in his early years growing up in a Quaker family. "This was a part of his upbringing that people help people; it's not the government's job to help people." Hoover said, "A voluntary deed is infinitely more precious to our national ideas and spirit than a thousandfold poured from the Treasury."

Hoover's seeming unresponsiveness made people believe he didn't care. Kohan adds, "He was not an emotional man in public. He was a very caring and wonderful man but people didn't know this; they didn't know a lot of the things he had done." In fact, from the time he had organized European relief during World War I, he didn't accept for his private use any salary for public service. He banked his presidential salary and gave it to charity. But in difficult times, it didn't seem to matter. Comedian Will Rogers even joked, "If someone bit an apple and found a worm it, Hoover would get the blame." In the 1932 election, Franklin Roosevelt soundly defeated Hoover.

Herbert Hoover was out of the public eye for much of the next decade, but when World War II erupted in Europe, he was once again active in bringing aid to those in need, much as he had done thirty years earlier. In the United States, he is still tagged with much of the blame for the Great Depression, but elsewhere that is not necessarily the case. Kohan notes, "Throughout the world he is revered so much more than he is in this country. They remember how much he did for them."

> " I think everyone who comes here is surprised to learn about his very full life outside of the presidency and the contributions he made," says Kohan. It's an important story for Americans to hear. While many still think of the dark days of the depression, it is Hoover who spent much of his life and his money helping others. His life's purpose was exemplified when he said, "A voluntary deed is infinitely more precious . . ." It is a value that guided President Hoover's life and it remains an example today.

Hot Dogs Fit for a King

Hyde Park, New York

> "I know that he had real fear when he was first taken ill, but he learned to surmount it. After that I never heard him say he was afraid of anything."

> —Eleanor Roosevelt of
> her husband Franklin

Did you know Franklin Roosevelt . . .

...Served hot dogs to a prominent world leader?

...Was paralyzed by polio when he was thirty-nine years old?

...Gave Americans confidence through a fireside chat?

He was related to eleven former presidents, either by birth or through marriage. His family was wealthy and he had always lived in a fine home overlooking the Hudson River. During his youth, he took vacations to Europe and was introduced to the leading men and women of the time. He was afforded an education at the best schools. Franklin Delano Roosevelt had the makings of a man who could have been completely out of touch with the vast majority of Americans, yet it was this man who perhaps best understood the needs of his countrymen during one of their most difficult times.

Roosevelt was born on January 30, 1882, at the family home in Hyde Park, New York, a place he would call home for his entire life. In 1905 he married Anna Eleanor Roosevelt and quickly entered the field of politics, earning a state Senate seat in 1910. By 1920, he was nominated for vice president of the United States, running on the Democratic ticket with James Cox, but the two lost to Warren Harding.

1921 was a year that affected FDR for the rest of his life, and it was a year that may have prepared him for what lay ahead for the country. In 1921 he contracted polio, a disease that at the age of thirty-nine rendered his legs and hips paralyzed. From then on, he used a wheelchair and leg braces to help him remain mobile. At that time, such men and women were at a huge disadvantage, without many of the conveniences that assist the physically challenged today. Many people would, in a sense, have given up.

His wife Eleanor saw how the challenge was actually preparing him for what lay ahead. "I know that he had real fear when he was first taken ill, but he learned to surmount it. After that I never heard him say he was afraid of anything," she said. He did not let this new challenge keep him down, as he was elected governor of the state of New York in 1922. In 1929 the stock market crash signaled the beginning of the Great Depression, yet FDR held on to his governorship in the 1930 state election, a time when many other elected officials lost their races. Already FDR had implemented programs in the Empire State to bring relief and security to citizens, and the electorate voted to keep him as governor.

In 1932 Franklin Delano Roosevelt was elected president of the nation and he quickly set about the work of restoring confidence in the country. He may not have known what would pull the nation from its depression, but he knew he couldn't idly stand by and do nothing. He said, "One thing is sure. We have to do something. We have to do the best we know how at the moment. If it doesn't turn out right, we can modify it as we go along." Soon programs such as the National Labor Board, the Civilian Conservation Corps, the TVA, the Works Progress Administration, Social Security, and the National Recovery Administration were helping Americans find work. A federal bank holiday was declared and the FDIC was established to restore confidence in banks.

When Roosevelt was inaugurated in 1933, he was leading a nation that had many fears. People feared for their own well being. They feared what might happen to their children. They feared they might not have a job, or even be able to get a job. Over a decade earlier, was it perhaps FDR's battle with polio that helped him empathize with people's fears now? Upon inauguration he delivered the famous line, "We have nothing to fear but fear itself." He also initiated his "fireside chats," the first of which was delivered over the radio on Sunday evening, March 12, 1933. Many Americans still refer to those broadcasts as if the president had sat down in their own living room simply to talk and reassure them. Although he had grown up in a home with few wants, he seemed to truly understand the needs of others. Roosevelt said, "It is an unfortunate human failing that a full pocketbook often groans more loudly than an empty stomach."

Their Springwood home in Hyde Park, New York, was a place to get away from the city, but even it seemed too crowded and busy at times for the president. In 1938 FDR had a home called Top Cottage built on top of Dutchess Hill, near his Springwood residence. Frank Futral, a curator at the Roosevelt-Vanderbilt National Historic Site of which the FDR homes are a part, says Top Cottage was a place to get away and relax. "Franklin said he built Top Cottage 'to escape the mob,' to get away from the pressures of the war."

Although many guests and dignitaries were accommodated at the larger and more formal home down the hill on the banks of the

Hudson River, Top Cottage occasionally served this purpose as well. One of the most memorable of those times was when the Roosevelts hosted King George VI and his wife Elizabeth. "They wanted to show the king and queen of England a slice of rural American life and that's why they chose to serve hot dogs," says Futral. In fact, the king said, "These are great; what are they?" Eleanor simply responded, "Hot dogs!" The king replied, "Great! I'll have another." The queen was less enthusiastic, however, and is reported to have only eaten a couple of bites of her hot dog.

When Roosevelt died on April 12, 1945, many Americans lost the only president they had ever known. They had lost the man who had spoken to them from beside the fireplace . . . the man who had helped ease their fears and had given them hope. Mike Autenrieth, ranger at Roosevelt's Springwood home, speaks of the impact the four-term president had on the country: "For so many Americans growing up in those difficult times, when he did pass away, for many young people especially, he was the only president they had ever known in their lifetime, so there was a tremendous love for him and he was truly missed."

Franklin Roosevelt once said, "The test of our progress is not whether we add more to the abundance of those who have much; it is whether we provide enough for those who have too little." He understood fear and he had learned to overcome it. His ability to not only relate to the needs of others but, most importantly, to help fill those needs and ease their fears, is why FDR is often regarded as one of the nation's best presidents. Our ability to understand the needs of others and provide the hope that conquers fears is also critical in creating lasting change.

The Buck Stopped Here

INDEPENDENCE, MISSOURI

*"When I first came to Washington, for the first six months,
I wondered how the hell I ever got here. For the next six months,
I wondered how the hell the rest of them ever got here."*

—HARRY TRUMAN

Did you know Harry Truman . . .

...WAS THE ONLY TWENTIETH CENTURY PRESIDENT WITHOUT A
COLLEGE EDUCATION?

...OFTEN KEPT A STEP AHEAD OF THE SECRET SERVICE AGENTS
PROTECTING HIM?

...READ ALL THE BOOKS IN HIS LOCAL LIBRARY?

Just looking at the situation on paper, Harry Truman appeared to
be in over his head. He was the only president in the twentieth
century not to have earned a college degree. He had been vice president for a mere eighty-two days when he was thrust into the White
House upon the death of Franklin Roosevelt. He had only two meetings with Roosevelt during that time and was not privy to many of
the details of Roosevelt's plan for winning World War II. He would

have to make a decision about dropping a nuclear bomb on Japan, although he most likely had no knowledge of the project before Roosevelt died in office.

But when you dig into the life of Harry S. Truman, you quickly realize that this man may very well have been the *most* qualified man to lead the country through the end of the war and to make the difficult decisions that came with the office. What on the surface appeared to be a lack of education and information was more than offset by a tenacious work ethic and personal integrity.

Born in 1884 in Lamar, Missouri, Truman's family later settled on a farm in Grandview (today on the outskirts of Kansas City). It was there, working the land, that he learned the values by which he would lead his life and lead the nation. He once said of his time plowing in the fields, "I've settled all the ills of mankind one way or another while riding along seeing that each animal pulled his part."

In 1910 while Truman was visiting his aunt and uncle, he had a chance meeting with his future wife. When his aunt gave Truman a cake plate to return across the street to the Wallace Home, Bess Wallace opened the door and thus began a nine-year courtship. Truman had known Bess for most of his life, and the two had even shared the same Sunday school class at the age of five and attended school together in Independence.

Carol Dage, museum curator at the Harry S. Truman National Historic Site in Independence, Missouri, says the time on the farm and his service in World War I had a great impact on his future. "He had learned on the farm, where he was from 1906 to 1917, that . . . he could lead men. He found out in World War I just how well he could do that." Captain Truman proved he was an effective and respected leader in battle, just as he had been at home.

In great part a self-educated man, to say Truman was an avid reader is a gross understatement. The fact that he read so much made up for the lack of a college diploma. Dage reflects, "They said that on the farm 'if he wasn't readin' he was figurin.'" He set out to learn all he could about every subject, whether it was crop rotations early in life or how to govern a nation upon the death of Franklin Roosevelt. Truman even stated in his memoirs, "By the time I was thirteen or fourteen years old, I had read all the books in the Independence Public Library." In 1902, the year after Truman's high school graduation, that library contained about three thousand books.

When he returned home from the war he married Bess Wallace and opened a haberdashery, a men's clothing store, with his friend Edward "Eddie" Jacobson. The business failed in 1922, but Dage says Truman handled the situation differently than others might have. "Harry Truman, as a man of integrity, spent many years paying that debt off, and he finally did pay it all. It was very important for him to maintain a good name and integrity in business and his personal life."

Truman found his way into politics, working his way up from a judge in Jackson County to become one of Missouri's senators. Franklin Roosevelt asked him to be his running mate in 1944, and with Truman's help won an unprecedented fourth presidential term. However, less than three months into his term, on April 12, 1945, President Roosevelt collapsed and died at his retreat in Warm Springs, Georgia. Harry S. Truman was sworn in as the nation's thirty-third president at 7:09 that evening. He had met with the president only twice since inauguration day.

Truman remembered back to his days on the farm when he met with reporters the next day. "Boys, if you ever pray, pray for me now," he said. "I don't know if you fellows ever had a load of hay fall on you, but when they told me yesterday what had happened, I felt like the moon, the stars, and all the planets had fallen on me."

By August 6 of that year, President Truman had made the decision to drop an atomic bomb on Japan. Dage says World War II veterans still come to the home and speak of the decision that probably saved the lives of thousands of troops who would have been needed for an invasion of the Japanese mainland. "It just sends chills through you to hear them say, 'If it hadn't been for Truman I wouldn't be here today,' and that happens time and time again." Truman didn't shirk from decision-making and he didn't blame others. The sign on his desk read "The buck stops here" and that's what he meant.

After leaving the White House in 1953, the Trumans returned to their home at 219 N. Delaware in Independence. Truman was an avid walker and could often outpace those assigned to protect him. He said, "As part of my daily routine I usually take a walk of a mile and a half at a pace of 120 steps a minute . . . If you walk 120 paces a minute, your whole body gets a vigorous workout." Secret Service agents found that Truman, now in his seventies, could "outwalk" just about anybody.

I've worked here for about thirteen years, and no matter who I've worked with, no matter who you talk to, his honesty and integrity always come through," says Dage. "Those traits were a part of his heritage and every aspect of his life. There was never any doubt about where he was coming from, who he was, and what he was about."

Truman's integrity and responsibility still speak to Americans today. When debts led him to declare his business a failure, he worked to eventually pay off those bills. When tough decisions had to be made, he made them and took responsibility for the consequences. When Franklin Roosevelt's death led him to the presidency, he rose to lead the nation through World War II. No doubt, these qualities were first learned riding the plow in the fields on the Grandview farm and he lived by them his entire life. As it turned out, the farm boy from Missouri who read all the books the library could offer ended up making what is arguably the biggest decision of the century.

Full Circle
KING CITY, MISSOURI

"Do what you can, with what you have, where you are."

— THEODORE ROOSEVELT

I was just two months old when Harry Truman passed away in Kansas City, yet his legacy was still very present as I grew up on our family farm in northwest Missouri. Much as the farm had affected Truman, I also learned life lessons while plowing fields, yet my work came on a tractor rather than behind a team of mules. Even as I visited my grandparent's home just a mile down the road from my own, I was greeted by a picture of President Truman hanging in the hallway just inside their front door. It only made sense that in 1984 when an essay contest was held to honor the one hundredth anniversary of Truman's birth, I decided to write about the man of whom so many Missourians had spoken. I received plenty of help from my mother as we penned the lines for that sixth grade essay.

It was a national event, and I don't think I finished anywhere close to first place in the contest. Nonetheless, the school received a beautiful framed centennial engraving of the president that was posted in the elementary school. It was displayed near the door to the principal's office (could it perhaps have been an ominous warning that "the buck" stopped there?), but years later it was taken down when renovations were made. My mother, who teaches fourth grade at the elementary school, asked if she could place it in her classroom since the framed engraving was destined for storage.

I cannot find the essay I wrote, yet the legacy for entering that contest remains via that engraving hanging on the classroom wall. Similarly, although the people I have written about in this book have passed, the legacy of their actions remains. Their service to the nation continues to impact us and their stories still serve as inspiration. Just as Theodore Roosevelt said, "Do what you can, with what you have, where you are," stories of the presidents continue to motivate us to live full lives.

When I embarked on this journey to visit at least one presidential site of all the presidents, I never imagined how much I would learn and grow. Each site seemed to have its own story, a legacy of a leader that unfolded to reveal lessons useful for today. It was a trip that went far beyond Washington, Jefferson, and Lincoln to uncover equally inspiring yet lesser known stories of other presidents. I hope you will also decide to take a detour to visit such sites and allow their stories to impact you.

Although I don't consider my journey to have ended, I do see the beginnings of that trek at my old elementary school. I realize that my presidential journey began in a second grade classroom where I memorized the names of the presidents and was rewarded with presidential trading cards from Mrs. Herbster. And when I occasionally stop by my mother's fourth grade classroom to visit with her students about some of my latest travels, I can't help but look at that plaque of Truman and wonder . . . wonder if perhaps another student may just be beginning a journey that brought me full circle, right back to the school from which I began to share with others the stories of my presidential journey.